HIS[TORIC]
AIR[SHIPS]

by RUPERT SARGENT HOLLAND
Illustrated by MANNING *de*V LEE

MACRAE · SMITH · COMPANY
Publishers ::: Philadelphia

Printing Statement:

Due to the very old age and scarcity of this book,
many of the pages may be hard to read due to the
blurring of the original text, possible missing pages,
missing text and other issues beyond our control.

Because this is such an important and rare work, we
believe it is best to reproduce this book regardless of
its original condition.

Thank you for your understanding.

Colonel Charles A. Lindbergh piloting the *Spirit of St. Louis*
in the first non-stop flight from New York to Paris

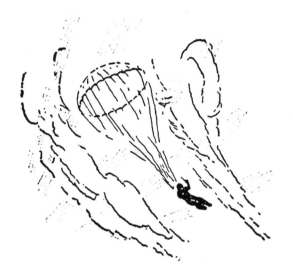

To
ALLAN M. SMITH AND EDWARD SHENTON

PREFACE

Many of those who have played leading parts in the history of airships—either as inventors or as aviators—have written books describing their achievements. Such books are most valuable to those interested in aeronautics and the author of this book has found them of great service. A volume of particular interest in the field of balloons is Aeronautical Prints and Drawings by W. Lockwood Marsh, which is beautifully illustrated; and two books which the author has found of exceptional use for their full treatment and entertaining style are Conquering the Air by Archibald Williams and Heroes of the Air by Chelsea Fraser.

FOREWORD

By

COMMANDER RICHARD E. BYRD

Two great duties, I think, we owe to posterity: one is progress, the other history. Only the former can we share in. The fruits of progress often apply to the generation which bears them. But the records of that progress come closer to being pure charity than any form of charity I know.

When an art or a science is born and developed with the rapidity of aviation the world is in a sense too stunned to get a good perspective on its advance.

So it is that I believe "Historic Airships" fulfills a real duty for the present and carries a message of inspiration for the future. It deserves a place in the library of every American who realizes the profound significance of man's mastery of the air. Surely no student of aeronautics should be without it any more than a young aspirant to the pilot's seat.

R. E. Byrd

List of Contents

List of ILLUSTRATIONS

CHAPTER I

FIRST VOYAGES
IN THE AIR

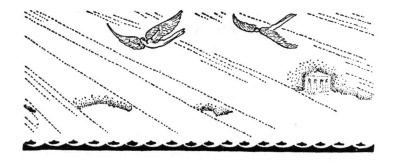

I

FIRST VOYAGES IN THE AIR

AMONG the legends of Greece is the story of Dædalus and Icarus and their flight from the island of Crete. For Minos the king it was that Dædalus, a famous inventor, fashioned a labyrinth in which to imprison the Minotaur. This feat of the clever artificer won the royal favor, but afterwards Dædalus incurred the enmity of Minos and was imprisoned by him. Dædalus, facile in invention, cast about for a means of escape; his solution was to make wings for himself and his son Icarus from feathers, which he fastened on with wax. Warning Icarus not to fly too near the sun, the inventor and his companion soared into the air high above the sea. On their left they passed Samos and Delos, on their right Lebynthos; then Icarus, exulting in his wings, forgot his father's caution and rose upward to the sun. The heat of that fiery orb melted the wax that held the wings to his shoulders, off they came, and down dropped the boy into the sea, which from his name is called Icarian.

21

Such is the Greek legend. Through the ages men, watching the birds, have pondered the problem of flight through the air by some sort of wings, but for long such as attempted to imitate Dædalus met with the downfall of Icarus instead. Men were not built like birds; to fasten on wings was not enough; he who would fly must be able to navigate the currents of the air as sailors navigate the ocean.

Leonardo da Vinci, the great Italian painter of the fifteenth century, who tried his hand at many things, studied this question of aerial navigation and made sketches of a machine that was to be driven through the air by flapping wings; these wings, something like those of a bat, were to spread out on the downward stroke and fold up on the upward stroke. Clever as Leonardo was—and this proposed machine of his was probably the best attempt made up to that time—this device was not practicable and one of its chief defects was that it provided no method of balancing from side to side. To Leonardo, however, belongs the credit of inventing the parachute, not in the umbrella form that was so much used later, but rather constructed like a framed, horizontal sail.

Francesco Lana worked out the plan of an aerial ship, in which the air was to be exhausted from metal spheres fastened to a boat. The boat was to be supplied with oars and sails for propulsion and steering, and the inventor proposed to create the vacuum in the metal spheres by filling them with water, which would drive out the air, and then let the water run out. His notion was that if a tap were closed at the proper time both air and water would be excluded and a vacuum obtained. This remarkable ship was never constructed, and if it had been it certainly would never have flown. Other inventions of flying machines are recorded—most of which never got beyond the point of being sketched or modeled—but it is probable that none of them ever actually ascended and sustained themselves in air until the first experiments with the balloon.

It was in the later half of the eighteenth century that two brothers, Joseph and Etienne Montgolfier, who were wealthy paper manufacturers of Annonay in the French province of Auvergne, became interested in balloons. According to one story their attention was directed to this field through having read an account of the experiments of Tiberius Cavallo, an Italian philosopher who was living in England. Cavallo had filled large soap-bubbles with "inflammable air," the name that was then given to hydrogen gas, had found that the bubbles so filled floated longer than ordinary soap-bubbles, and had published a treatise on the subject. The Montgolfiers had often observed how clouds hang in the atmosphere and they thought that if a body of vapor or of smoke could be enclosed in a large bag the bag might be able to lift itself high in air. Cavallo's treatise perhaps first interested them in the use of hydrogen gas, for they tried this in a balloon they constructed of paper. They soon gave up inflammable vapor, however, as it escaped through the pores of the paper almost at once.

Turning their attention to other methods of inflation, they built a small paper balloon with an opening at the bottom and lighted pieces of paper below it. Thereupon the balloon, according to an account of the experiment, "began to distend itself, and in a few minutes sustained itself by being held at its lower part; when, on being released, it ascended to the ceiling of the chamber, where it remained a few minutes, much to the joy and astonishment of its projectors. Moved by this pleasing experiment, they next tried it in the open air. Here again, after it was inflated and released, it ascended, reaching a height of about 70 feet."

The Montgolfiers then constructed a bag of spherical shape and with a capacity of about 600 cubic feet. This balloon, inflated in the same manner as the first, was so powerful that it broke the strings that held it to the ground and rose to a height of some 600 or 700 feet. Next a bigger balloon was built, 35 feet in diameter and with a capacity of 23,000 cubic feet. The experimenters had found that paper alone was incapable of holding the hot air and so they made the envelope of paper lined with fine linen. This balloon was given a trial on April 25, 1783; it ascended to a height of 1,000 feet and travelled almost a mile before it came to the ground.

Delighted with these successes, the Montgolfiers issued invitations to a public exhibition in the mar-

ketplace of Annonay on June 5, 1783. There a sceptical crowd of townspeople watched the huge bag
distend above a fire of straw and wool that was lighted
in a pit under its neck. At a signal the ropes were
cast off and, marvel of marvels! the throng saw the
balloon rise up and up to a height of 6,000 feet and
sail away a mile and a half from the marketplace.

Word of the wonderful ascension at Annonay
spread far and wide and Etienne Montgolfier was
invited to go to Paris, there to lecture before the
Royal Academy of Sciences and repeat his balloon
demonstrations. For this purpose he built a new balloon, 72 feet high, 41 feet in diameter, and weighing
about 1,000 pounds. This he exhibited before the
members of the Academy in Paris on September 12,
1783, and the balloon took up with it a load of between 400 and 500 pounds.

Montgolfier was the hero of the hour. At the royal
command he took his balloon, to which he had now
attached a small wickerwork basket, to Versailles
for a demonstration on September nineteenth. Louis
XVI and his queen, Marie Antoinette, with many
of their court, were present. In order to test the
safety of the balloon for passengers a sheep, a cook
and a duck were placed in the basket. A wooden
staging had been built; beneath this a fire was
lighted for rarefying the air, and the balloon was
placed over an opening in the centre. When the bag
was inflated it was released with its three passengers;
up it went to a height of 1,500 feet, stayed in the air

for eight minutes, and landed in Vaucresson Wood, about two miles from where it had ascended. The sheep, the cock and the duck arrived on terra firma uninjured and this initial success decided Montgolfier to build a larger and more solidly constructed balloon to carry human passengers.

This new balloon was a gorgeous affair, decorated in blue, with the signs of the Zodiac, the royal cipher and other designs in gold. The opening at the bottom was fifteen feet across and was surrounded by a wickerwork gallery with a balustrade on the outside. In the neck there were holes through which the passengers were to throw bundles of straw onto an iron brazier suspended from the orifice by chains and so replenish the fire in order to renew the hot air and keep the balloon inflated.

François Pilâtre des Roziers, having made several ascents up to 300 feet in "captive" balloons, volunteered to make the first "free" flight. On this first free ascension of human passengers he was accompanied by a friend, the Marquis d'Arlandes. The great event took place on November 21, 1783, from the Château de la Muette, the residence of the Dauphin. This is the story in the words of the official account:

"Today, November 21, 1783, at the Château de la Muette [in the Bois de Boulogne] took place an experiment with the aerostatic machine of M. de Montgolfier. The sky was partly clouded, the wind northwest. At 8 minutes after noon a mortar gave notice that the machine was about to be filled. In 8 minutes, notwithstanding the wind, it was ready to set off, the Marquis d'Arlandes and M. Pilâtre des Roziers being in the car. It was at first intended to retain the machine awhile with ropes to judge what weight it would bear, and see that all was right. But the wind prevented it rising vertically, and directed it towards one of the garden walls. The ropes made some rents in it, one of six feet long. It was brought down again and in a short time was set right. Having been filled again, it set off at 54 minutes past one, carrying the same persons. It rose in the most majestic manner and when it was about 270 feet high, the intrepid voyagers took off their hats, and saluted the spectators. No one could help feeling a mingled sentiment of fear and admiration. The voyagers were soon indistinguishable; but the machine, hovering above the horizon, and displaying the most beautiful figure, rose at least 3,000 feet high and remained visible all the time. It crossed the Seine below the barrier of La Conference; and, passing thence between the École Militaire and the Hôtel des Invalides, was in view of all Paris. The voyagers, satisfied with this experiment, and not wishing to travel further, agreed to descend; but seeing that the wind was carrying them upon the houses of the Rue de Sêve, they preserved their presence of mind, increased the fire, and continued their course through the air till they crossed Paris. They then descended quietly on the plain, beyond the new Boulevard, opposite the

Mill of Croulebarbe, without having felt the slightest inconvenience, and having in the car two thirds of their fuel. They could, then, if they had wished, have gone three times as far as they did go, which was 5,000 toises [about 1¾ miles], done in from 20 to 25 minutes.''

That is the contemporary account of the first authenticated voyage ever made by man through the air.

In making the voyage these first aeronauts frequently threw fuel on the fire to replenish the hot air and keep the balloon from descending. Their adventures were graphically described in a letter written by the Marquis d'Arlandes to a friend. After relating the incidents of the first part of the trip he says: "I heard a new noise in the machine, which I thought came from the breaking of a cord. I looked in and saw that the southern part was full of round holes, several of them large. I said: 'We must get down.'

'' 'Why?' [asked Pilâtre des Roziers.]

'' 'Look!' said I.

"At the same time I took my sponge and easily extinguished the fire which was enlarging such of the holes as I could reach, but on trying if the balloon was fast to the lower circle I found it easily came off. I repeated to my companion: 'We must descend.' He looked around him and said, 'We are over Paris.'

"Having looked to the safety of the cords, I said:

'We can cross Paris.' We were now coming near the roofs. We raised the fire and rose again with great ease. I looked under me and saw the Mission Étrangères, and it seemed as if we were going towards the towers of S. Sulpice, which I could see. We rose, and a current turned us south. I saw on my left a wood, which I thought was the Luxembourg. We passed the Boulevard, and I called out: *'Pied à terre!'*

"We stopped the fire, but the brave Pilâtre, who did not lose his self-possession, thought we were coming on to some mills and warned me. We alighted at the Butte aux Cailles, between the Moulin de Merveilles and the Moulin Vieux. The moment we touched land I held by the car with my two hands. I felt the balloon press my head lightly. I pushed it off and leaped out. Turning towards the balloon, which I had expected to find full, to my great astonishment it was perfectly empty and flattened."

The Montgolfier balloons—or "Montgolfières," as the hot air balloons were called,—had a rival in the field that autumn of 1783. A professor of physics at Paris, J. A. C. Charles, constructed a small balloon and, making the bag air-tight by a coating of India rubber, filled it with hydrogen instead of hot air. He was assisted in this work by the brothers Robert, and the experimenters gave a demonstration of their hydrogen balloon at the Champs de Mars on August 27, 1783. The balloon, which weighed about nineteen pounds and had a capacity of 940 cubic feet, rose to a height of some 3,000 feet, and was then engulfed in clouds. Having floated ten miles, it fell in the village of Gonesse, where the peasants, thinking it a dangerous monster of some new sort, attacked it with weapons and then tied it to the tail of a horse and dragged it across country. To reassure the public a proclamation was issued forthwith that explained the construction of the new balloon and added that "anyone who sees one of these globes, presenting the appearance of an obscured Moon, may be satisfied that so far from being a terrifying phenomenon, it is only a machine . . . which is quite harmless and which it is to be presumed will some day prove of benefit to Science."

Professor Charles and his assistants then built a larger hydrogen balloon with a car for passengers. This balloon had a valve at the top that was worked by ropes from the basket so that passengers might regulate the escape of gas when they wished to descend. On December 1, 1783 a crowd of 600,000 spectators collected in the Tuileries gardens to watch the ascent of this balloon, which was called a "Charlière." Charles and one of the Robert brothers were to make the trial trip. Before he stepped into the basket Charles handed to Montgolfier a small balloon. "It is for you, monsieur," he said, "to show us the way."

This graceful compliment—a tribute to the successful voyage of Roziers in a Montgolfière a few days before—was received by the throng with cheers.

The Charlière—made of alternate gores of red and yellow silk, with a net over the bag to provide support for the basket, a valve to regulate the gas, a barometer, and sand-ballast—had a close resemblance to the modern balloon. The car was well stocked with ballast and the aeronauts' friends had thoughtfully contributed some wine and warm clothing. A cannon was fired as signal for the start of the second voyage made by aeronauts.

When the balloon had risen to 1,800 feet, according to the barometer, the gas-valve and ballast were used in order to keep the Charlière on a horizontal course and in view of the Parisians. Without misadventure the voyagers sailed away and presently, when all the ballast had been thrown overboard, descended in the plain of Nesles. Here the travellers were greeted by admiring country people and a report of the trip was signed by several clergymen and magistrates. The Duc de Chartres rode up and embraced both the aeronauts; then M. Robert got out of the car and Professor Charles made another ascent by himself. The balloon again worked perfectly and made a second successful landing.

Charles made no other ascensions, although his hydrogen gas balloon had thoroughly justified itself. His method, however, rather than Montgolfier's was adopted in later balloon voyages. Presently hydrogen gas, which was very expensive, was replaced by the coal gas that was used for lighting.

Montgolfier continued with his hot air or fire balloons. He built one with a capacity of nearly half a million cubic feet; the exterior of the balloon was very ornate and was painted with representations of mythological heroes. This was constructed at Lyons and there were many who wanted to make a trip in it when it was ready to ascend on January 19, 1784. As soon as it had been inflated four young noblemen—Prince Charles de Ligne, and the Comtes de Laurencin, Dampierre and Laporte—jumped into the car, drew their swords and defied anyone to put them out.

Montgolfier and Pilâtre des Roziers wanted to ascend, and so Roziers suggested that the six should draw lots and so choose three for the trip. The four noblemen, safely in the basket, answered the suggestion by cutting the mooring ropes with their swords. As the balloon started to rise Montgolfier and Roziers scrambled aboard and so did a man named Fontaine, who had helped in the building. Seven passengers sailed up in the basket while the people of Lyons danced with delight.

The Montgolfière set off famously, but soon gas escaped from the bag through a rent of four feet or more where the fabric had been damaged by fire and not properly repaired. Down went the balloon and struck the ground rather violently. The passengers escaped without injury, however, and at the opera that evening were given a public ovation.

On June 23, 1784 Roziers and a friend, M. Proust,

made a voyage in a fire balloon, the *Marie Antoinette,* from Versailles. On this trip the aeronauts ascended above the clouds and attained an elevation of 11,732 feet, which is probably the greatest height ever reached by a Montgolfière. As they sailed they were able to rise and descend as they wished and made a safe landing forty miles from their point of departure, having been the first to travel above the clouds.

The Montgolfiers and Charles had successfully demonstrated the use of the balloon for travel in the air.

CHAPTER II

JOURNEYS BY BALLOON

II

JOURNEYS BY BALLOON

AN adventurous character—one Mr. J. Tytler —is credited with being the first to ascend in a balloon in the British Isles. This pioneer rose from the Comely Garden, Edinburgh, on August 27, 1784, in a fire balloon, but as he had no apparatus for replenishing the hot air in the bag the voyage was a short one; a mile from the garden the hot air was dissipated and Tytler perforce landed.

An Italian, Vincent Lunardi, the secretary to the Neapolitan ambassador, was the first balloonist to attract public attention in England. He built a balloon, 33 feet in diameter, the fabric, of alternate red and blue stripes, being varnished with oil. In this he planned to ascend with a friend, a Mr. Biggin, from the grounds of the Honourable Artillery Company outside London on September 15, 1784. Lunardi had provided his balloon with oars, with which he thought he might be able to control direction, but the balloon had no valve to regulate the escape of gas.

Lunardi wrote an account of his enterprise, and in this he says: "The impatience of the multitude made it inadvisable to proceed in filling the balloon, so as to give it the force it was intended to have. On balancing the force with weights, it was supposed incapable of taking us up. When the gallery was annexed and Mr. Biggin and I got into it the matter was beyond doubt, and whether Mr. Biggin felt the most regret in relinquishing his design, or I in being deprived of his company it may be difficult to determine. But we were before a tribunal, when an instantaneous decision was necessary; for hesitation and delay would have been construed into guilt, and the displeasure impending over us would have been fatal, if in one moment he had not had the heroism to relinquish, and I the resolution to go alone.''

A smaller gallery was substituted for the original one, and Lunardi was about to start when someone reported an accident to the balloon. This injury was trifling, however, and the spectators were impatient. Therefore, continues Lunardi, ''I threw myself into the gallery, determined to hazard no more incidents that might consign me and the balloon to the fury of the populace, which I saw was on the point of bursting. An affecting testimony of approbation and interest in my fate was here given. The Prince of Wales and the whole surrounding assembly almost at one instant, took off their hats, hailed my resolution, and expressed the kindest and most cordial wishes for my safety and success.''

A gun was fired, the ropes were cast off, and the balloon rose with the aeronaut and his companions, a pigeon, a dog and a cat. ''On discharging part of the ballast,'' Lunardi says, ''the balloon ascended to a height of 200 yards. As the multitude lay before

me, all the 150,000 people who had not seen my ascent
from the ground, I had recourse to every stratagem
to let them know I was in the gallery, and they liter-
ally rent the air with their acclamations and applause. In these stratagems I devoted my flag, and
worked with my oars, one of which was immediately
broken and fell from me.''

As the balloon rose higher the air became cold, so
that, in his own words, he ''found it necessary to take
a few glasses of wine. I likewise ate the leg of a
chicken, but my bread and other provisions had been
rendered useless by being mixed with the sand which
I carried as ballast.''

After voyaging for almost an hour and a half he
descended in a cornfield in South Mimms. Here he
landed the cat, which was shivering with cold, but as
a crowd had gathered to watch his wonderful exploit
he threw out some ballast and ascended again. He
wrote a letter, tied it to a corkscrew and chucked it
overboard, also some plates, knives and forks, and an
empty bottle. Presently the balloon came down at
Standon, in Hertfordshire, where some farm-hands
were at work in a field. ''I requested their assistance''; says Lunardi, ''they exclaimed they would
have nothing to do with one who came in the Devil's
house, or on the Devil's horse—I could not distinguish which of the phrases they used—and no en-
treaties could prevail on them to approach me. I at
last owed my deliverance to the spirit and generosity
of a female. A young woman, who was likewise in

the field, took hold of a cord which I had thrown out, and calling to the men, they yielded that assistance to her request which they had refused to mine."

All England echoed with Lunardi's fame. The balloon was exhibited in London, where thousands paid to see it, the king gave him a reception, a purse was subscribed for him and a medal struck in his honor. Afterwards he went to Scotland, where he made a number of successful voyages and on one of these sailed through the air for more than one hundred miles.

The balloon, thanks to Lunardi, became popular in Great Britain and a number of ardent aeronauts went soaring through the air. Voyages lengthened, and presently a Frenchman who had made several flights, Jean Pierre Blanchard, proposed to attempt to cross the English Channel in a balloon. On one of his trips he had taken a well-to-do American, Dr. John Jeffries, with him as passenger, and when Jeffries heard that Blanchard was planning to be the first to voyage over the open sea he offered to pay all the expenses of the flight—estimated at some £700— if Blanchard would take him along.

The start was to be made from Dover in December, 1784, but the weather was unpropitious for some weeks and the attempt was postponed. Meantime Blanchard, perhaps moved by the wish to win all the glory for himself, put obstacles in the way of Jeffries, and even went so far as to increase his own weight by wearing a loaded belt, so as to prove that

In 1783 the Montgolfier Brothers' hot air balloon made its
first ascent in the Bois de Boulogne

the balloon could not carry two aeronauts in addition to the ballast. Jeffries, who had put up the money, insisted on Blanchard's keeping his bargain and was supported in his contention by the Governor of Dover Castle. Blanchard ultimately agreed, and on January 7, 1785, the weather and wind being favorable, though the air was very cold, the balloon was inflated for the ascent. Jeffries' report says: "The balloon being filled a little before one o'clock, we suffered it to rise, so as to be disengaged from the apparatus, etc., for filling it, and to be drawn down again right to the edge of the cliff, where we attached the oars or wings with the moulinet and gouvernail to the car. Exactly at one o'clock (having in the car with us three sacks of sand ballast of ten pounds each, a large parcel of pamphlets, two cork jackets, a few extra clothes of M. Blanchard, a number of inflated bladders, with two small anchors or grapnels, with cords affixed, to assist our landing) we rose slowly and majestically from the cliff, which being at the time of ascent from it almost covered with a beautiful assembly from the city, neighbouring towns and villages, with carriages, horses, etc., together with the extensive beach of Dover, crowded with a great concourse of people, with numbers of boats, etc., assembled near the shore, under the cliffs, afforded us, at our first arising from them, a most beautiful and picturesque view indeed."

The "oars or wings" mentioned by Jeffries were part of Blanchard's regular balloon paraphernalia;

what the "moulinet and gouvernail" were is a subject of doubt.

The balloon travelled smoothly at the start, but when it was about one-third of the way across the Channel it descended so fast that half of the ballast had to be thrown overboard. It rose again, then again it dropped; the rest of the ballast and some of the pamphlets were tossed out. Half way across the balance of the pamphlets were thrown over, but still the balloon was too heavy. "At about half past two," states Jeffries, "I found we were descending very rapidly. We immediately threw out all the little things we had with us, such as biscuits, apples, etc., and after that one of our oars or wings; but still descending, we cast away the other wing and then the gouvernail; having likewise had the precaution, for fear of accidents, while the balloon was filling, partly to lessen and make it go easy, I now succeeded in attempting to reach without the car, and, unscrewing the moulinet with all its apparatus, I likewise cast that into the sea. Notwithstanding all which, the balloon not rising, we cut away all the lining and ornaments, both within and on the outside of the car, and in like manner threw them into the sea. After which we cast away the only bottle we had taken with us."

Even the ornaments and the bottle were not enough; the aeronauts began to throw their clothing into the sea; then they put on their cork jackets in anticipation of the balloon dropping to the water, now close beneath the basket.

The shore of France was some four or five miles distant when, as the car almost touched the waves, an upward current of air caught the balloon and swept it on and over the French coast at three o'clock in the afternoon. The aeronauts, stripped of most of their clothes and shaking with cold, took off the cork jackets and, as the balloon began to descend in a large forest, threw the jackets overboard. Rising a little distance, the voyagers caught at a tree and working along from branch to branch managed to steer the balloon above a clearing in the woods. The valve in the bag was then opened and the balloon came safely down to the ground in the forest of Guines, near Calais.

The travellers were warmly welcomed, and the following day at a public meeting Blanchard received the freedom of the city of Calais. The French king summoned him to Paris and rewarded him with a gift of £500, besides a pension of £50 a year and other emoluments. Dr. Jeffries was given the freedom of Dover in recognition of his part in the first balloon voyage from England to France.

The intrepid Pilâtre des Roziers, first to ascend in a balloon, attempted to duplicate this voyage across the English Channel later in that year. His plan was to travel from Boulogne to the coast of England in a double balloon, an extremely hazardous enterprise.

With a grant from the French Government of £1,600, he built a hydrogen balloon and below it hung a fire balloon to which the car was attached. His idea would seem to have been that by varying the ascent of the fire balloon he might do away with the necessity of throwing out ballast or allowing the gas to escape from the hydrogen bag. So rash appeared this project that his friends, among them Professor Charles, tried to dissuade him from making the experiment, telling him that he was putting flames beside powder. He insisted on trying his plan, however, and after waiting at Boulogne some time for favorable weather, rose with his brother in the double balloon from French soil on June 15, 1785. As they ascended a French nobleman threw a purse of 200 louis into the car to pay for a seat, but the aeronauts declined to take him with them.

The balloon rose to 700 feet, and then a current of air deflected its course and blew it inland. The spectators watched intently and saw that the two voyagers were busy with the fire basket; presently a blue flame shot forth and in the twinkling of an eye the balloon was wrapped in fire. Down crashed the balloon and the car, striking the earth almost on the spot where Blanchard and Jeffries had safely arrived a few months before; both the voyagers were killed, and Pilâtre des Roziers, the first aeronaut, was thus one of the first victims of aerial travel.

Many voyages of considerable length were made by balloon, and ascensions by aeronauts became a popular feature of outdoor entertainments. Information was collected in regard to the temperature and moisture of the atmosphere at various heights and the thickness of cloud strata, as well as of the velocity and direction of wind currents. Daring trips were attempted, and some of the most interesting of these were the voyages made from Paris after the German army had encircled the French capital in September, 1870.

It was almost impossible for the French to send messengers out from the city, so vigilant was the German blockade, and in this predicament the government in Paris adopted the use of balloons in order to keep in communication with the outside world. These balloons were made of calico that was rendered airtight by a dressing of oil or paint. Almost daily a balloon rose and sailed away over the walls of Paris.

The Frenchman in charge of this aerial service, Felix Tournachan, better known under the assumed name of Nadar, had his fill of excitement in one of the attempts he made to carry government dispatches from Tours to Paris. He set out from Tours at six in the morning and by eleven o'clock was near the capital city, flying at a height of some 10,000 feet. Sighting another balloon, Nadar displayed the French flag, whereupon the other aeronaut responded by showing the same tricolor. The two balloons, now moving in the same air current, drew close together, and then the stranger unfurled the German flag and opened fire on the Frenchman. Nadar returned the fire, and so successfully that his opponent was driven off and the Frenchman was able to land safely within the walls of Paris, to the great delight of the crowds who from the city had been watching what was probably the first aerial combat that had ever been fought.

A very large balloon, christened *La Bretagne,* started from Paris on October 27, 1870, to try to reach London. The wind carried it to the northeast at first, but then the breeze veered to the west and blew directly towards the territory occupied by the Germans. Dense clouds enwrapped the balloon and the four aeronauts in the car were unable to make out their position; then, suddenly, through a rift in the clouds they caught sight of German troops marching underneath them. Immediately they threw out ballast and the balloon rose high in air. On they travelled until they judged they must have passed the frontier of Belgium; thereupon they released gas and the balloon came down quickly, so quickly indeed that it struck the ground with a crash. One of the aeronauts jumped out when the balloon was 40 feet in air; he landed in a newly-ploughed field and was unhurt, but was immediately captured by German soldiers.

The balloon bounded up again, while bullets rained around it, and some of these probably struck it, for it came down shortly in a field near Verdun. Two of the three aeronauts who had made this second ascent jumped out and were taken prisoner by the enemy. Again the balloon rose, with its single passenger, M.

Manceau, and easily soared to an elevation of 10,000 feet. Then rain commenced to fall, and Manceau, becoming dizzy, let out some of the gas and the balloon descended. Before it landed Manceau leaped out and fell with such force in a quagmire that he dislocated his right ankle. In spite of that, however, he managed to hide the balloon and then to crawl on all fours to the dwelling of a priest.

This priest contrived to smuggle the dispatches over the Belgian border, but the wounded aeronaut was betrayed by a villager to the enemy and Manceau, like the three companions with whom he had set out from Paris, spent the rest of the war as a prisoner of the Germans.

The success of these balloon voyages from the besieged city depended of course largely on the direction of the wind. Two aeronauts left Paris on November 24, 1870 in an attempt to reach Tours, but their balloon ran into a strong gale from the south and was blown to the northeast and over the sea. After voyaging a long distance they came to the ground in a country covered with snow and inhabited apparently only by wolves. Trudging through drifts, they at last found a house and learned to their amazement that they had been carried more than six hundred miles in thirteen hours and were in Norway!

CHAPTER III

SANTOS-DUMONT

III

SANTOS-DUMONT

THE balloon would voyage through the air, but only in the direction and at the speed of the air currents in which it floated. It was, in a sense, like a raft which has neither oars nor sail nor rudder and which moves on a stream therefore entirely as the currents of the water propel it. To make it really serviceable for journeys a method of steering the balloon must be devised and to stimulate interest in air navigation Henri Deutsch, a member of the French Aero Club, in 1900 offered a prize of one hundred thousand francs to the first person who should voyage through the air from the Aero Club Park around the Eiffel Tower and back to the starting-point, and make the journey in half an hour.

The challenge was accepted by Alberto Santos-Dumont. This aeronaut, a Brazilian by birth and son of a rich coffee-planter, had come to Paris in 1891 and made a study of balloons. At first he experimented with one of spherical shape and very small dimensions; to make it as light as possible he used thin Japanese silk as the material for the bag, an innovation in construction. Having practiced with this, he turned his attention to the building of a balloon that should be dirigible.

Automobile tricycle motors were then being perfected and Santos-Dumont decided to adopt one of these light but powerful motors for his balloon. He had great difficulty in getting suitable workmen, but at length succeeded in fashioning a balloon 82½ feet long and holding 6,300 cubic feet of gas. From this he hung a wickerwork basket with a 3½ horsepower motor. The rudder he made of silk stretched over a triangular steel frame. He also had two bags of ballast, one fore and one aft; these were suspended from the balloon-envelope by cords, and could be drawn in towards the basket if it were desired to trim the balloon.

This airship—the Santos-Dumont No. 1—was ready for its trial trip on September 18, 1898. It rose successfully from the Jardin d'Acclimatation in Paris, but almost immediately encountered the branches of some trees which injured it so that it had to descend. Two days later it ascended again; this time it sailed over the trees without misadventure; to quote Santos-Dumont's own account of this trip: "Under the combined action of the propeller impulse, of the steering-rudder, of the displacement of the guide-rope, and of the two sacks of ballast sliding backward and forward as I willed, I had the satisfaction of making my evolutions in every direction—to right and left, and up and down."

Rising high above Paris, he steered towards the Longchamps racecourse, and, emboldened by success, threw out ballast until he reached a height at which a considerable amount of gas escaped by expansion. When he started to descend the balloon, which was in the shape of a long cylinder, began to fold up like a pocket-knife, the tension of the cords became unequal, and those which now carried all the weight threatened to tear loose. The balloon was coming down rapidly when Santos-Dumont, catching sight of some boys on the ground, called to them to grasp the end of the guide-rope and run with it against the wind. This they did, and by their help the velocity of the fall was lessened and Santos-Dumont was enabled to land uninjured.

The next year he built another airship, the Santos-Dumont No. 2, larger than the first one and with a little aluminium ventilator to ensure permanency in the form of the balloon. On the day of its first trip, after the balloon had been filled with hydrogen gas, rain began to fall; rather than empty out the hydrogen the aeronaut decided to ascend, but no sooner had he risen than the wetness caused a great contraction of the hydrogen and the balloon commenced to shrink. A strong gust of wind doubled it up, and threw it into the tree-tops, which finished the career of the Santos-Dumont No. 2.

In November of that year he made a very successful flight in the Santos-Dumont No. 3. Steering over the Champs de Mars, a clear, open space, he experimented in various forms of aerial navigation, driving ahead in a straight course, circling, turning diagonally upward and downward, and acquiring a very satisfactory mastery of shifting-weights. These experiments led him to state that he believed the central truth of dirigible ballooning was to descend without sacrificing gas and to mount without sacrificing ballast.

The Santos-Dumont No. 3, after a number of successful trips, was discarded, as the inventor considered its balloon too clumsy and its motor too weak. He had now built his own aerodrome and gas-plant, and planned to construct a larger and better airship than the first three. A great exposition was to be held in Paris in 1900, and in September the International Congress of Aeronautics was to meet there; Santos-Dumont determined that he would have his airship No. 4 ready to demonstrate.

No. 4 was a decided improvement on its predecessors and he made almost daily flights with it during August and September of the exposition year. These trips suggested new improvements, especially in the type of motor and in the form of airship keel, and these were embodied in the new Santos-Dumont No. 5, which he now set about building.

The Deutsch prize for the first aerial flight from the Aero Club Park around the Eiffel Tower and back had now been announced, and Santos-Dumont constructed his airship No. 5 with the intention of trying to win the prize with it.

Having tested his new airship and found it much more powerful than the others, Santos-Dumont invited the committee of the Aero Club to see him make a flight from the Club grounds at Saint Cloud early in the morning on July 13, 1901. He started off at 6.41 A. M., rounded the Eiffel Tower in ten minutes, and came back against an unexpected headwind, reaching the time keepers of the Club at Saint Cloud forty minutes after starting, at an altitude of 200 meters, and after a tremendous struggle with the gale. At this point the motor stopped, and the airship, without the service of its engine, drifted and fell on the tallest chestnut tree in the park of Edmond de Rothschild. The aeronaut was perched in the tree while the propeller of the airship touched the ground beneath. The balloon was not much damaged, but all the gas had escaped from the bag.

The Princess Isabel, Comtesse d'Eu, daughter of Dom Pedro, the former Emperor of Brazil, lived in a near-by villa, and when she heard that Santos-Dumont would be some time disengaging his airship from the branches she sent lunch to him in his tree and invited him to come and tell her of his trip. When Santos-Dumont had related the adventures of his flight the princess said; "Your evolutions in the air make me think of the flight of our great birds of Brazil. I hope that you will do as well with your propeller as they do with their wings, and that you will succeed for the glory of our common country!"

A few days later the princess sent him a medal of St. Benedict to protect him against accidents, and this the aeronaut wore on a gold chain around his wrist, an ornament that was often referred to as Santos-Dumont's "bracelet."

When the airship No. 5 was repaired Santos-Dumont made several practice trips and then again, on August 8, 1901, invited the officers of the Aero Club to watch him make a second attempt to win the prize. Starting early in the morning, he made the turn around the Eiffel Tower in nine minutes and headed back towards Saint Cloud. On this return journey hydrogen escaped from the balloon and the bag flattened; by the time the airship reached the fortifications near La Muette the suspension wires were sagging so much that those nearest to the screw-propeller caught in it as it revolved. Santos-Dumont instantly switched off the motor, which left the balloon at the whim of the wind, and it was swept back towards the tower. The balloon was falling, now half-empty of gas the nose of the airship was tilting upward and the unequal strain on the suspension wires seemed likely to break them and allow the car to crash to the ground.

Beneath were high buildings. These were almost safely cleared when the end of the balloon that still held some gas slapped smartly against a roof and exploded with a great noise. The aeronaut then found himself suspended in his wicker basket high up in the courtyard of one of the Trocadéro hotels, supported by the keel of the airship which stood braced at an angle between the courtyard wall and the roof of another building lower down.

Santos-Dumont in His Dirigible No. 5

The *Los Angeles* and Smaller Blimps in the Hangar

Firemen at the station at Passy had been watching the airship and when they saw it fall they hurried to the rescue of the stranded aeronaut; a rope was lowered from the hotel roof, Santos-Dumont caught hold of it and was pulled up to safety, then the balloon was extricated, a jumble of strips and fragments and suspension wires.

That was the last voyage of airship No. 5. Twice Santos-Dumont had tried a flight for the Deutsch Prize and each time he had rounded the Eiffel Tower, which he himself considered the most difficult feature of the trip, since an error in steering or some chance side-wind might dash his ship against the tower, yet each time the balloon had met with an accident on the homeward leg of the course. He was not to be daunted, however, and on the day of his fall in the hotel courtyard he ordered another airship—the Santos-Dumont No. 6—which was completed in twenty-two days.

This new airship was larger than any of its predecessors; the capacity of the balloon was 22,239 cubic feet, and it carried a four-cylinder motor of 12 horsepower. The aeronaut tested it in a number of flights, was satisfied with its performance, and on October 19, 1901 made his third try at the Deutsch Prize. At 2.42 P. M. the airship ascended. The wind struck the balloon sidewise but Santos-Dumont held his course straight to his goal, the Eiffel Tower. Up he went, aiming to attain a considerable distance above the top so as to secure himself against accidental contact with the tower. As he passed the tower he swung the rudder about, bringing the airship round the lighting-conductor on the tower's top, and at nine minutes after starting the flight was pointing his nose towards home. The wind was now against him; moreover he had not gone far on the return stretch when the motor seemed actually on the point of stopping.

He had to decide quickly. What he did was to leave the steering-wheel for a moment, at risk of drifting from the course, in order to attend to the carbureting lever and the lever that controlled the electric spark. The motor then began to work again; so on the airship sailed until it was over the Bois, where the cool air from the trees made the balloon heavier and heavier; then the motor slowed, and the airship commenced descending while at the same time the motive power was decreasing.

To offset this descent Santos-Dumont threw back both the guide-rope and the shifting-weights. This made the airship point diagonally upward and the force of the propeller sent it mounting in the air. It was now over the Auteuil race-track, where a great throng were watching, and the cheers reached the aeronaut's ears. There the motor started working at full-speed again, the airship seemed to point her nose amazingly high, and at this the applause of the crowd changed to cries of alarm. Soon they saw that the airship was under control and their interest became centered on the question whether the goal could be reached in the time limit of a half-hour.

Santos-Dumont righted his course by shifting the guide-rope and the weights forward and sped rapidly along. At a high altitude he passed over Longchamps, crossed the Seine, and dashed on over the heads of the officials in the Aero Club's grounds. He made the goal in twenty-nine minutes and thirty seconds. Going at full-speed he flew past the judges, then slowing down, turned and came back where eager hands caught the guide-rope and checked the airship. "Have I won?" he called out.

The crowd below roared back: "Yes, yes, you've won!"

Hardly had he alighted, however, when a dispute broke out. The President of the Aero Club declared that he had not won the prize, since the time of his reaching the goal should be calculated to the moment when his guide-rope was caught after he had turned and not to the moment when he had sailed over the line high in air. Between the letting go of the rope at the start of the flight and the catching it at the finish more than thirty minutes had elapsed, although he had actually covered the distance in the time prescribed. For some days this point was argued; at length, however, the officers of the Aero Club pronounced that the prize had been won and Santos-Dumont received the award of one hundred thousand francs, which he divided between the poor of Paris and the workmen in his airship shops.

From the government of Brazil he also received

an award of one hundred and twenty-five thousand francs and a gold medal. On the design of the medal was a line from the Portuguese poet Camoens. Camoens' words read: "Through seas heretofore unsailed." The line on the medal was: "Through heavens heretofore unsailed"; and this line Santos-Dumont adopted as the legend to float on the pennant of his airships.

This resourceful and intrepid aeronaut, pioneer in the field of the dirigible balloon, built many more airships, which became a familiar sight in the heavens above Paris. He aroused so much interest in aerial navigation in France that he may rightly be regarded as the founder of French air fleets. Later he studied and built aeroplanes and in one of them made one of the first flights in Europe in a heavier-than-air machine driven by a gasoline motor.

In the story of aviation Santos-Dumont played a leading part; he was the first to use an internal combustion motor in an airship.

CHAPTER IV

BUILDING WINGS

IV

BUILDING WINGS

THE idea of flying through the air on wings had long fascinated men of inventive minds and many had attempted to work out a practicable method. In the forefront of these experimenters stands the Englishman, Sir George Cayley, a Yorkshire squire, who is called the "Father of Aerodynamics." In 1809 and 1810 he published descriptions of experiments he had made with aerial gliders. For these gliders he advocated the use of wings with curved, rather than flat, surfaces, and also the use of fixed supporting surfaces instead of the flapping devices recommended by other inventors. He made mention of a glider he had built on which he had sailed from the top of a hill at a gentle angle, and suggested that if an internal combustion engine should be used considerable distance ought to be attained.

Cayley aroused much interest in this new field of a heavier-than-air flying machine. His experiments were presently further developed by William Samuel Henson and John Stringfellow, who worked together at Chard, in Somersetshire. Hanson actually designed and took out a patent on a miniature flying-machine which had a single supporting surface and two aerial screws which were driven by a steam engine. This he did in 1842, and then organized a company which was to carry passengers, mail and parcels through the air in his machine. In his patent he speaks of his invention as having "a very extended surface or plane of a light yet very strong construction, which will have the same relation to the general machine which the extended wings of a bird have to the body when the bird is skimming through the air; but in place of the power for onward progress being obtained by movement of the extended surface or plane, as is the case with the wings of birds, I apply suitable paddle-wheels or other proper mechanical propellers worked by a steam or other sufficiently light engine, and thus obtain the requisite power for onward movement to the plane or extended surface."

The big machine to be used for commercial purposes was not built, but Henson and Stringfellow constructed some very clever models, and Stringfellow, who was an adept at turning out light steam-engines, built in 1848 a small, self-propelled flying-machine, weighing 8½ lbs, that sustained itself in the air. The pioneer work of these two inventors was supplemented by the experiments of a number of others, one of whom, F. H. Wenham, working out a model with long, narrow planes placed one above another, demonstrated that the longer a plane was in relation to its fore and aft width, the greater its lifting power would be.

It was almost a century, however, after Cayley's

description of his aerial gliders before what might be termed an actual, workable aeroplane was devised. This was accomplished by Professor Samuel Pierpont Langley, the Secretary of the Smithsonian Institution at Washington, who began his studies of the subject in 1887. He built a model that was remarkable for its mechanical craftmanship; what might be termed a double monoplane, having a large plane in front and a second plane of almost the same size at the back and at the same level as the front one. Below the planes hung a body that was shaped like a boat so that it might rise from and alight in water; and in this body there was an engine and boiler which could develop from 1 to 1½ horsepower. This model Langley launched from a houseboat on the Potomac River and it rose against the wind and sailed through the air for about three-quarters of a mile at a speed of between 20 and 25 miles an hour. When the supply of naphtha in the engine gave out the model descended to the water. Much elated at this success, Langley built a larger machine with an engine capable of furnishing 52.4 brake horsepower. With this he made two trial flights in 1903, but in each case the machine caught on the launching apparatus and was wrecked. Langley's experiments proved that one horsepower could maintain at least 20 lbs. in the air and that proper balance could be secured by a right arrangement of the planes. His achievements attracted much attention and his writings carried the knowledge of aerodynamics a long step forward; some years later an authority on aviation, Dr. A. F. Zahn, after comparing a modern machine with one of Langley's, declared "Langley had every equipment needed for a steady flight of many hours in fair weather, but he never got a chance to rise and demonstrate it."

A successful airplane—even if a very primitive one and having many defects from a later point of view—had been constructed, and experimenters in aerial flight were now busy along many different lines.

Cayley, the great pioneer, had diligently studied the flight of birds and had learned that birds are lifted by the air as they move forward from a running start. In his glider, therefore, a man simply took hold of the wings and ran down hill against the wind, and of this glider he said that it supported a man "so strongly as scarcely to allow him to touch the ground, and would frequently lift him up and carry him several yards together. It was beautiful to see this noble white bird sail majestically from a hill to any given point of the plain below it, with perfect steadiness and safety." To his pair of wings he attached a tail or rudder, since he had observed that a bird uses its tail to balance its body fore and aft.

This plan of Cayley's of learning how to fly by gliding through the air on a pair of wings seemed to many later experimenters a much safer method of studying flight than to imitate Langley's use of engine-driven machines. A great student of birds,

Mouillard, a Frenchman, built a glider that consisted of a pair of wings with a rudder and a handle-bar; holding the handle-bar he would run along the ground until the upthrust of air against the wings lifted him and carried him upward.

Another experimenter, Otto Lilienthal, a native of Anklam, in Pomerania, followed the same line. Lilienthal stated in 1896: "Experiments in gliding by a single individual, following closely the model of bird gliding, is the only method which permits us, beginning with a very simple apparatus and in a very incomplete form of flight, to develop gradually our proficiency in the art of flying." He studied the methods of young storks in learning to fly and saw that they always practised facing the wind and not with it behind them. His training as an engineer was a great help to him, and he started his experiments in gliding by using a pair of rigid outstretched wings that were fastened to each other and to a tail. There was an opening between the wings for the flyer's body. This glider weighed about 50 lbs. and had a sustaining area of 160 square feet. The wings were made of cotton twill stretched on a light framework of willow wood and were curved fore and aft.

Putting his head and arms through the central opening and gripping the edges, he faced the wind and ran down a hill until the glider lifted him from his feet. The strength of the wind mainly determined how far he could glide before touching earth again. Balancing he found difficult; his method when the machine tilted to one side was to throw his weight over to the other side in an attempt to right it, a proceeding that gave him the appearance, as he swung his legs about and twisted and squirmed, of trying to swim through the air. For his experiments he found a conical mound, about 50 feet in height, that sloped gently on all sides, thus enabling him to glide in whichever direction the wind happened to be blowing.

Lilienthal persevered with his glider until he had succeeded in making flights of three hundred yards. Sometimes he was able to soar higher than the starting-point and also to change his course by moving his body so as to shift the centre of gravity. In order to increase the length of his flights he constructed a biplane glider, which had some 200 square feet of surface; this, however, was much heavier than the monoplane and far more difficult to balance.

His next step was to equip his monoplane glider with a small engine that was driven by carbonic acid gas, intended to flap movable parts of the wings. Before he made a trial flight in this motor-driven machine he took one of his gliders out to try a new rudder in a high wind, lost his balance, and falling from a height of 100 feet was almost instantly killed.

An English marine engineer, Percy S. Pilcher, had visited Lilienthal at Berlin and been much interested in his work. He built gliders of the Lilienthal type, but he sat between the wings instead of hanging from them and also added an under-carriage on wheels. To start a flight his machine was pulled along the ground by a line and a multiplying gear until the monoplane rose, when the line was cast loose. He placed the gear on a hill overlooking a valley and the glider on another hill facing the first so that gravity aided it in gaining velocity. With this contrivance he made glides of 250 yards. Then one day when he was giving an exhibition flight the tail of his glider broke and from his fall Pilcher sustained fatal injuries.

Pilcher contributed two new ideas: the launching of a glider with a rope and gear, and the value of an undercarriage to lessen landing shocks.

In the United States two engineers, Octave Chanute and A. M. Herring—the latter a pupil of Lilienthal—were experimenting with gliders on the shores of Lake Michigan. They wanted to obtain some better method of balance than Lilienthal had achieved, and therefore they built gliders with as many as five surfaces, one above the other, and these they found were steadier and safer than Lilienthal's. Their greatest success was obtained with a two-surfaced glider, or double-decker, in which the planes were connected by struts and wires so that they could withstand strong winds without injury. The pilot of a Chanute biplane had to shift his weight as Lilienthal had, but not nearly so much, and he could fly in more violent winds than those attempted by Lilienthal or Pilcher.

While these men were experimenting with gliders

there were others who were working on the idea of steam-driven machines. One of the most notable of these was Clément Ader, a French electrical engineer, who had made a fortune so that he might devote it to the experiments in air flight. Like Mouillard, he studied birds; Dr. Zahn says of Ader in his book "Aerial Navigation": "Going to Algeria, he disguised himself as an Arab, and with two Arab guides, journeyed to the interior where he watched the great soaring vultures, which he enticed with bits of meat to perform before him their marvellous manœuvres, wheeling in wide circles, and without wing beat, from earth to sky."

In France Ader built an engine-driven monoplane, which he christened the *Éole,* and in which, according to his own statement, he flew 150 feet on October 9, 1890. In another machine he said that he flew 300 feet. The wings of these Ader monoplanes were very much arched and pointed at the ends and the machine was given motion by a steam-driven propeller. They looked like enormous bats, especially the plane he built—called the *Avion*—with the financial help of the French War Department. In return for this aid the inventor was obliged to conduct his experiments in secret and this has made it difficult to substantiate his accounts of flights. It is claimed, however, that he travelled through the air some hundreds of yards in the *Avion* on October 11, 1897, which would give him the credit of having made the first actual flight in a flying machine.

This flight apparently ended in the destruction of the machine; the War Department lost interest in the experiments, and the inventor, through lack of funds, had to retire from the field.

High in the annals of invention stands the name of Hiram Maxim, a man born in Maine who spent most of his time in England. Among other things he invented the machine-gun, and his ingenuity and astuteness in all fields of mechanics were most remarkable. Turning to the subject of flying machines, he experimented for several years with propellers, lifting surfaces, and the problems of air resistance. Then he constructed a boiler and engine that should develop a great deal of power in relation to their weight. The machine he presently built had its engines mounted on a platform that was attached to a framework, which had fastened to it a large central upper plane with smaller planes stretching out on each side. Two other small planes were attached at a lower level, so that the machine was in effect a biplane, with an elevating plane in front of the main one and a tail plane behind it. The sustaining surface was about 4,000 square feet and with three passengers aboard the machine weighed 8,000 lbs. In comparison with Ader's machines this one of Maxim's was indeed a giant, and not until Glenn H. Curtiss built the *America* for a flight across the Atlantic Ocean in 1914 was any bigger airplane constructed.

When Maxim's flying machine was built—it is said

at a cost of $100,000—his next step was to devise a method by which such a great machine could be made to rise from the ground. For this purpose he built a steel track half a mile long on which he could run the airplane and outside this he laid guard-rails to prevent the machine from rising, since he wished to test it thoroughly before attempting to fly. On board the machine he installed apparatus for measuring the lifting power of the planes and the pushing force of the propellers.

The airplane's first run on this track was made with a boiler pressure of 150 lbs. to the square inch, and all the lower wheels remained in place on the inner rails. On the next run the boiler pressure was increased to 240 lbs., and at that speed the machine lifted but was kept on the track by the guard-rails. Maxim then had the airplane fastened to a dynamometer for measuring pull, and raised the pressure to 300 lbs. Full steam was turned on and the propeller thrust rose to nearly a ton. The inventor gave the word to let go and the machine started forward so vigorously that it almost threw the crew off their feet.

"The first part of the track," Maxim wrote in his account of this memorable achievement, "was up a slight incline, but the machine was lifted clear of the lower rails and all of the top wheels were fully engaged on the upper track when about 600 feet had been covered. The speed rapidly increased,

and when 900 feet had been covered, one of the rear
axletrees, which were of 2-inch steel tubing, doubled
up and set the rear end of the machine completely
free. . . . The rear end of the machine, being set
free, raised considerably above the track and
swayed. At about 1,000 feet the left forward wheel
also got clear of the upper track, and shortly afterwards the right forward wheel tore up about 100 feet
of the upper track. Steam was at once shut off, and
the machine sank directly to the earth, embedding
the wheels in the soft turf without leaving any other
marks; showing most conclusively that the machine
was completely suspended in the air before it settled
to the earth. . . . The total lifting effect upon the
machine must have been at least 10,000 lbs."

This trial trip of Maxim's on July 31, 1894, although it was less than a quarter of a mile in length,
was an outstanding event in the history of aeronautics, for then for the first time man was actually
lifted into the air on wings by mechanical power.
Hiram Maxim had accomplished what many inventors had been attempting for many years, a feat
that many engineers and scientists deemed impossible. He had spent so much money on his experiments up to this point that he could not afford to
continue them further; had be been able to do so
he very probably would have achieved even greater
triumphs.

The glider and the flying machine had been carried far forward by the studies and experiments of Lilienthal, Pilcher, Chanute, Herring, Langley, and Maxim. Next to come on the scene were two Americans, the famous brothers Wilbur and Orville Wright.

CHAPTER V

WILBUR AND ORVILLE WRIGHT

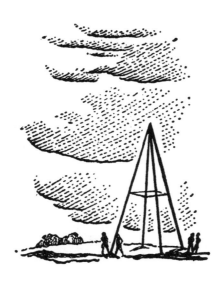

V

WILBUR AND ORVILLE WRIGHT

WILBUR and Orville Wright, the first to demonstrate the actual use of heavier-than-air, passenger-carrying airplanes, were natives of Dayton, Ohio, sons of the Reverend Milton Wright, a bishop of the creed of the United Brethren in Christ, a man of very fine and inspiring character. An accident on the playground made an invalid of Wilbur just when he was preparing to enter Yale, and he stayed at home, helping his parents. There was plenty to do in that household; the father's income was not large, and, although two of the older children had married and set up homes of their own, there were still in the minister's simple dwelling Wilbur, his younger brother Orville and younger sister Katherine.

There are interesting glimpses of the family life. One evening the father came home with a small toy in his hands, which he tossed into the air, whereupon it flew up to the ceiling. The toy was what the scientists call a helicopter, but what the Wrights dubbed a bat. It greatly interested the boys and they played with it until it came apart. Then they became interested in accounts of polar exploration and especially in the adventures of Robert E. Peary;

then they became absorbed in making furniture and
ornaments with carving and engraving tools. Bicycles became the popular rage and Wilbur, now
strong again, joined Orville in starting a small bicycle shop in Dayton. They repaired bicycles and
they built them; one of a type they constructed and
called the Van Cleve became very well known in
Ohio. Then, in 1896, when Wilbur was twenty-nine
and Orville twenty-five, they heard how the German
inventor, Lilienthal, while experimenting with his
glider, had crashed to the ground. That accident set
the brothers to wondering what was wrong with Lilienthal's machine, and presently one of them said to
the other, "Let's try to make a glider that WILL fly."

They had previously experimented a good deal
with kite-flying and had made some small helicop-
ters or bats that would screw themselves up in the
air; now they read all the literature on aviation that
they could find. Chanute had demonstrated in his
work on the shores of Lake Michigan that gliding
was safe in his type of machine, so the Wrights
turned their attention to Chanute's glider. They saw
that the defect in his machine was that the pilot had
to shift his weight somewhat in order to maintain
a proper balance, though not nearly so much as Lilienthal had had to do; their first problem therefore
became how to obtain a better method of maintaining balance than any yet devised.

For their experiments they wanted some place

where winds of sufficient velocity blew frequently and steadily, not strong winds but constant ones, to enable them to work without interruption. They asked the Weather Bureau where the most constant winds were to be found in the United States and the answer came: "In Dare County, North Caroline, on the seacoast. Kitty Hawk, just north of Cape Hatteras, always has a wind."

To Kitty Hawk, in North Carolina, on the Atlantic Coast, the Wright brothers went, and there in October, 1900, they began their active experiments. The glider they used was intended to be flown like a kite, with a pilot aboard, and in winds blowing from 15 to 20 miles an hour. Experiments showed, however, that much stronger winds were required to lift the machine, and so, in the absence of such winds, the Wrights flew the glider without a pilot on board and worked the levers that controlled the balance by cords held by the experimenters on the ground. This enabled them to prove to their own satisfaction the reliability of the method they had invented to maintain the balance of a glider in the air.

This method invented by the Wrights for maintaining balance in the air was what made the aeroplane a successful flying machine. They had solved the problem that had baffled earlier experimenters, the problem of how to make the air itself bring the machine back on an even keel as it tilted from side to side, or in other words how to increase the air-pressure under the falling side of a wing and so raise it to the proper height.

What the Wrights did was to construct the wings of their machine so that they could be warped at the rear. When a wing tilted downward, the pilot pulled a cord or lever that bent the rear edge of the tilting wing; this caused that wing to offer more resistance to the air, which increased the air-pressure against it, and consequently the wing was forced upward. At the same time the pilot by using the cord or lever would bend up the rear edge of the opposite rising side so that there would be less surface for the air to press against and thereby make that side incline down.

This "warping of the wings," as it was popularly called, was what secured balance in the air, did away with the necessity of the pilot's shifting his weight, and made flying by airplane possible. The Wrights worked it out on a double-decker machine of the Chanute type, in which they made various improvements. They constructed their machine so that the pilot could lie flat on it, which exposed much less body-surface to the air than an upright position. Since this flat position made it difficult for the pilot to move about, they attached a horizontal rudder, or small plane, in front of the main planes, and by tilting this rudder the pilot was able to keep a proper balance fore and aft. To maintain the correct bal-

The Wright Airplane First to Make a Sustained Flight

Glenn Curtiss in One of His Early Planes

ance from side to side they used their device for warping the rear edges of the planes.

The next year, 1901, the Wrights returned to Kitty Hawk with a much larger machine, for which they built a shed. Chanute visited them at their camp at Kill Devil Hill, four miles south of Kitty Hawk, and watched their experiments. The new machine, with an area of 308 square feet, behaved erratically; the planes, it was found, were too much curved, but when they had been flattened somewhat the machine did much better and glided for distances of almost 400 feet.

In their third season at Kitty Hawk the machine used by the Wrights had planes longer and narrower than those formerly employed and behind them were fitted two fixed vertical tails intended to keep the machine steady. This glider worked very well, particularly after the tail had been made movable and served as a rudder. In September and October of 1902 the Wrights made some 1,000 gliding flights, several of which covered more than 600 feet, and some of which were accomplished against a wind of 36 miles an hour. On a number of these flights the machine and pilot stayed in the air for over a minute and the glider would soar a considerable time in one spot without any descent.

Having now thoroughly tested their method of maintaining balance, the Wrights in 1903 commenced to experiment with an engine-driven machine. Their first one was much like their gliders, but as it had to carry a much greater weight it was larger and more strongly built. There was a seat for the pilot in front of the planes and on either side was a lever for moving the front elevator, for warping the wings, and for controlling the steering rudder at the rear. To the bottom of the machine were fixed two skids to facilitate alighting on the ground.

The gasoline engine they built themselves, a somewhat clumsy and heavy affair, of 25 horsepower, and weighing, with its attachments, about 250 lbs. This they fastened between the planes at the same distance from the centre line as the pilot's seat, so as to secure balance sideways, and the engine was connected by chains with two large propellers that revolved in opposite directions behind the planes. The machine, with a pilot aboard, weighed some 900 lbs., and as it was therefore too heavy to be launched by hand like a glider the builders worked out another method.

This method was the use of an inclined track. A single rail was laid down on which ran a trolley that carried the flying machine. At one end of the rail was a wooden structure inside which a heavy weight was to be raised by gearing. From this weight a rope ran along the rail, round a pulley at the opposite end, and back to the trolley. The airplane was placed on the trolley and brought to the end with the weight; the weight was lifted, the rope fastened to the carriage; then the motor was set going, the retaining catch released, and the machine started forward, partly by its own engine-power and partly by the pull of the rope. When it reached the end of the rail the airplane had gained sufficient speed to send it soaring into the air.

The first trials of the new, engine-driven machine were made at Kitty Hawk. On these initial attempts the airplane would not fly and various alterations and repairs were needed. The Wrights then planned to make another trial on December seventeenth. Orville afterwards wrote: "There was a strong, cold wind from the north when my brother Wilbur and I went to bed at Kitty Hawk, N. C., on the night of December 16th, 1903. We arose next morning to find that the puddles of water left by the recent rain were covered with ice and that the wind was still blowing at a velocity of around 25 miles an hour.

"The necessary track was laid though not without difficulty, since the biting cold compelled us frequently to retire to a shed where a wood fire was burning in an old carbide can.

"Eventually all was ready. . . . A hand anemometer showed the velocity of the wind to be between 24 and 27 miles an hour. . . . I mention this because to-day, with a generation of aërial development and research to profit by, nobody, not myself at least, would dream of going up in a strange machine in a 27-mile wind, even if he knew that the machine had previously flown and was apparently sound.

"I ran the motor a few minutes to heat it up, and then released the wire that held the machine to a wooden track. The machine started forward, Wilbur helping to balance it by running alongside. With the wind against it, the machine got under way so slowly that Wilbur was able to stay alongside until it lifted from the track after a run of 40 feet.

"The flight lasted 12 seconds. Its course was rather erratic, owing in part to air conditions, in part to the pilot's inexperience. The front rudder was balanced too near the centre, so that it had a tendency to turn by itself, with the result that at times the machine would rise to about 10 feet and then as suddenly aim toward the ground. One of these darts ended the flight 120 feet from the point where the machine had first risen from the wooden track. . . . This was the first time in history that a machine carrying a man raised itself by its own power into the air in full flight, went ahead without reduction of speed, and landed at a point as high as that from which it started."

Five persons besides the Wrights witnessed this epoch-making flight on December 17, 1903. On that same day four other flights were made, and each time the machine stayed in the air a little longer. In the last flight it covered a distance of 852 feet in a little less than a minute.

The Wrights had succeeded in proving the ability of man to fly through the air.

The inventors now went on building machines with

various improvements and flying them sometimes at Kitty Hawk, sometimes in a field near their home in Dayton, Ohio. In 1904 they increased their record for duration in the air to 5 minutes, 17 seconds, covering a distance of over 3 miles. They also succeeded in making a circular flight. The following year they remedied various defects and achieved even better results, some of which they described in a letter they sent to the Aeronautical Society of Great Britain, in which they said:

"We have finished our experiments for this year after a season of gratifying success. Our field of experiment has been very unfavorable for experiment a great part of the time, owing to the nature of the soil and the frequent rains of the past summer. Up to the 6th. September we had the machine out on but eight different days, testing a number of changes which we had made since 1904, and as the result the flights on these days were not so long as our own of last year. During the month of September we gradually improved in our practice, and on the 26th. made a flight of over 11 miles. On the 30th. we increased this to 12 miles, on 3rd. October to $15\frac{1}{3}$ miles, on 4th. October to $20\frac{3}{4}$ miles and on the 5th. to $24\frac{1}{4}$ miles. All of these flights were made at about 38 miles an hour, the flight of the 5th. October occupying 38 minutes 3 seconds. . . . We had intended to place the record above the hour, but the attention these flights were beginning to attract compelled us to suddenly discontinue our experiments in order to prevent the construction of the machine from becoming public. The machine passed through all of these flights without the slightest damage. In each of these flights we returned frequently to the starting point, passing high over the heads of the spectators."

The Wrights, satisfied now that they had constructed a successful and very valuable flying machine, looked about for a purchaser for their invention, and offered it first to the United States Government. The government was not at that time interested in flying machines, so the inventors tried to find a market in Europe. England declined their proposal, and they turned to France, where aviation was attracting a great deal of attention.

In France a number of men were trying to fly and were making use of light gasoline-engines to propel their primitive airplanes. Santos-Dumont had built a machine that looked like a big box kite and had attached a rudder that enabled him to steer up and down and from side to side. He had not solved the problem of balance, but he gave a public exhibition in 1906 and flew 200 yards before a wildly applauding crowd. Other aviators imitated him, some in biplanes, some in monoplanes, and several of them succeeded in flying considerable distances in very quiet air, but none of them had learned the correct principle of balancing that the Wrights had discovered.

This was the situation when in 1908 Wilbur Wright began to give demonstrations of his machine

The Dirigible *Los Angeles* over a city at night

in France in the hope of selling his French patents. The French were sceptical of the reports of his achievements, but they opened their eyes in amazement when on September 21, 1908, he made a continuous flight of over an hour and a half at Le Mans. By his method of balancing he was able to perform remarkable evolutions in the air, climbing to heights none of the French flyers had achieved, and his rivals were quick to acknowledge the complete success of his invention for maintaining balance.

On December 31, 1908, Wilbur Wright won the Michelin prize and $4,000 and established a new world's flying record of 2 hours, 18 minutes, and 33 seconds; the official distance he covered was 77 miles and 760 yards, the actual distance, including turns, was about 95 miles; the longest flight yet made by a heavier-than-air machine. As a result of these exhibitions he sold his French patents to the Astra Company.

Meantime the United States Government was becoming interested and offered $25,000 for a machine that would make certain evolutions in the air and fly 125 miles, returning to its starting point and carrying two men. Orville Wright attempted to meet these conditions in the summer of 1909 at Fort Myer, Virginia. His first trials were unsuccessful, and various alterations were made in the machine. On the twentieth of July he set a new American record by flying for over 1 hour and 20 minutes. A week later he flew with a passenger for almost an hour and a quarter at a speed that averaged about 40 miles an hour. On July 30, 1909, he accomplished all the conditions specified by the government: on a straightaway course of 5 miles and return, carrying a passenger, he maintained a speed of something more than 42 miles an hour, and won the $25,000 and a bonus of $5,000 more.

With the acceptance of the Wright machine by the United States Government and the sale of their patents in France the crown of complete achievement may be said to have been set upon their work. They continued making improvements in design and construction; in 1910 they did away with the front rudder, which seemed to be responsible for a pitching movement; they also changed the method of launching the machine in air, and instead of starting it on an inclined rail they fastened bicycle wheels to the landing-gear so that the machine, after a flying start on the ground, would soar into the air under its own power and momentum.

Many experimenters, during a long course of time, had built up the airplane; the Wrights made it actually fly. The machine they demonstrated at Fort Myer was in most respects not very different from flying machines that others had constructed; it had two wings, one placed above the other—other inventors had done that; it had a horizontal rudder in front to steer it up and down—other machines had front rudders; there was a vertical rudder at the rear—but so had almost all earlier machines; a gasoline-engine between the wings propelled it—

such engines had been used many times; it had two propellers—propellers were no innovation. But the Wrights had invented a method of making their flying machine balance from side to side and in doing that had made possible practical human flight. That one all important solution of balance was their great contribution to aviation. Rightfully they deserve the proud fame of having created the airplane.

CHAPTER VI

THE FIRST AIRPLANE CROSSING
OF THE ENGLISH CHANNEL

VI

THE FIRST AIRPLANE CROSSING OF THE ENGLISH CHANNEL

THE English Channel is only twenty-one miles across at its narrowest point, but in 1909, when airplanes were still in their infancy and flights across open water had not been attempted, the idea of flying over the silver ribbon that divides England from the continent of Europe held great fascination for adventurous airmen. An English newspaper, the Daily Mail, offered a prize of £1,000 to the first aviator to make the trans-Channel flight. Two competitors appeared: Hubert Latham, a Frenchman of part English ancestry, and Louis Blériot, another Frenchman.

Latham had had considerable experience in flying an Antoinette monoplane, especially in stormy weather, before he took his machine to Sangatte, which is near Calais, in July, 1909. The *Harpon,* a French torpedo boat, had instructions to follow him and give aid if he got into difficulties. For some time Latham waited for favorable weather; on July nineteenth he judged that conditions were suitable and at 6.20 A. M. .signal guns announced the start of the flight. Down the slope to the edge of the cliff ran the Antoinette and rose into the air. Wireless sent the word to Dover and crowds on the cliffs of England looked expectantly across the water.

The *Harpon* set out in chase. Soon after leaving France the Antoinette had flown into a light cloud and vanished from the French watchers. Then it was seen again, making a direct line towards Dover. A second time the monoplane disappeared, and now the watchers thought that some accident must have befallen the daring aviator.

Presently in came the *Harpon* to the harbor of Calais, with Latham aboard. He had flown about 7 miles at a speed of almost 45 miles an hour when the engine commenced to misfire. The airplane then lost height and Latham had been obliged to glide down towards the water and meet it at as slight an angle as he could. This he managed so skillfully that, although the machine was going at a high speed when it struck the water, it rested easily on the surface and floated buoyantly, adequately supported by its hollow wings. There the *Harpon* came up with Latham, took him on board, and towed back the airplane, which was somewhat damaged, though its engine was intact.

Undiscouraged at the failure of his first attempt Latham immediately went to Paris to get a new machine, which a few days later arrived at Sangatte.

In the meantime Louis Blériot appeared at Les Barraques, another village near Calais. He had lately made a flight of 25 miles in a monoplane built to his own design, a very small and compact machine, weighing only 484 lbs. when empty, and with a three-cylinder engine of 25 horsepower. Inside the frame Blériot fitted a large air-bag intended to keep the machine floating in case it fell into the water.

The rival airmen were ready now and each eagerly watched the weather in order to be first away.

Storms blew across the Channel for several days, but when Blériot, who was restless because of an injured foot, which he had burned, looked from his window at 2.30 A.M. on the morning of July twenty-fifth he saw that the wind had dropped and the weather was favorable. Immediately he left his hotel, went to the tent where his airplane was housed, had it brought out, and as dawn was lighting the sky made a trial trip. The machine worked admirably, and he decided to start his flight to England.

At 4.35 in the morning Blériot gave the order to his mechanics to let go. The machine rose splendidly. "My course to the sea," Blériot said in a statement given to the London Times, "lay across the sand dunes, and then I had to surmount the telegraph wires which run along the coast. It was because I wished to be certain of clearing these that I started on the plain. I struck across the dunes and went over the telegraph wires at a height of about 180 feet. I could see the destroyer *Escopette* a few miles out at sea, and as she was to steam towards Dover I took my bearings from her. The destroyer was steaming at full speed, but I very quickly passed her. My machine was then travelling at about 45 miles an hour, the revolutions of the propellers being about 1,200 to 1,400 a minute. While travelling over the Channel my monoplane was at a height of about 250 feet. At times she dipped a little, but I always got her to rise again.''

For a while Blériot was able to steer his course by looking back at the destroyer and following the line of direction in which she was steaming; then the ship was lost to view and as the English coast was not visible the aviator adopted the plan of setting his steering gear for the point at which he had last seen the *Escopette* heading. For ten minutes he flew with only the sea and sky in sight. "It was the most anxious part of the flight," he said, "as I had no certainty that my direction was correct, but I kept my motor working at full speed and hoped that I would reach Dover all right. I had no fear of the machine, which was travelling beautifully. At last I sighted an outline of the land, but I was then going in the direction of Deal, and could see the long beach very plainly. In setting my steering I had overlooked for the moment the effect of the wind, which was blowing very strong from the southwest, and had therefore deflected me eastward. I could have landed at Deal, but I had started to come to Dover, and made up my mind to land there. I headed my monoplane westward, therefore, and followed the line of the coast to Dover about a mile or a little more out at sea. I could see a fleet of battleships in Dover Harbor, and I flew over these to a point where I could

Blériot Crossing the English Channel

The Antoinette Monoplane Which Fell into the Channel

see my friend, M. Fontaine, with a large French tricolor, denoting the point where I was to descend. I
flew in over the cliffs all right, but the descent was
one of the most difficult I have ever made. When I
got into the valley between the Castle and the opposite hill I found an eddying wind. I circled round
twice to ease the descent, but I alighted more heavily
than I had anticipated and the monoplane was
damaged.''

Blériot had flown across the English Channel by
airplane—the first man to do it—and had arrived
in the Northfall Meadow at Dover at such an early
hour in the morning that few people were up and
the only witness to his reaching the ground was a
policeman on duty at that point. Soon, however, the
word spread, and crowds came flocking to congratu-
late him; the news of his success was sent broadcast
and when he reached London by train from Dover
the streets were packed with cheering throngs welcoming the hero. The airplane was placed on public exhibition and within four days 120,000 people
went to view it. In France the enthusiasm was quite
as great; Louis Blériot was a national idol.

Blériot well deserved his great triumph. He had
studied aviation for years and had built many flying machines. One of these was a monoplane that was
nicknamed the ''Canard,'' because its shape resem-
bled that of a flying duck, with a long neck. The duck
would not fly, however, nor would several other of
the machines he built, and it is said that he had fifty

accidents in trying to fly, though in none of them, fortunately, did he meet with serious injury. He spent at least £20,000 in his experiments, but, as he himself declared, it was a greater thing to be the first to fly across the Channel than to win the £1,000 prize.

Latham was one of the first to send a message of congratulation to his successful rival. He had given orders when he went to bed on the night of July twenty-fourth that he was to be called at 3 A. M. the next morning if the wind seemed light enough for him to attempt a flight. The wind was light at that hour but through some oversight Latham was not called until some twenty minutes after Blériot had actually started. He then immediately made his preparations and got into his machine; by that time, however, the wind had increased so much that the flight could not safely be attempted.

Two days later the wind conditions were suitable and early in the morning Latham started in the Antoinette from the coast of France. A wireless message had been sent to Dover and the populace that had missed seeing Blériot fly to their shore gathered in thousands to welcome Latham. A flag at Dover gave the signal that he had started; after some ten minutes field glasses made out a dark speck over the water that came on and on until it looked like a huge bird. Loud were the cheers of delight as the monoplane came rushing on at what seemed tremendous speed. Then the Antoinette, which was flying a few hundred feet above the sea, commenced to circle round and lose height. Down it went until it struck the water less than a mile from the English shore. Immediately boats put out and Latham was taken on board a destroyer and landed at Dover, where he, fine sportsman, was given a royal welcome.

In the next year, on May 23, 1910, Jacques de Lesseps, a son of the great engineer who built the Suez Canal, flew from Les Barraques in France and landed after a flight of 37 minutes in an English meadow opposite the South Foreland lightship.

The first crossing by airplane in the opposite direction, from England to France, was made by the Hon. C. S. Rolls on June 2, 1910. He started at 6.30 P. M. in a Wright biplane from Dover, made a wide circle, and set out over the Channel at a good height. The flight across the water was safely accomplished, and at 7.15 P. M. Rolls was over French soil. His plan was to return to England without alighting, so he flew above the Channel Tunnel works near Sangatte, dropped three letters with greetings to the Aero Club of France, turned towards Dover and reached his starting place in England at 8.06 P. M. This achievement, crossing the Channel twice in about an hour and a half, was a feat worthy of record close to Blériot's historic trans-Channel trip.

CHAPTER VII

PIONEER LONG DISTANCE FLIGHTS

VII

PIONEER LONG DISTANCE FLIGHTS

THE English newspaper, the Daily Mail, did a great deal to stimulate interest in aviation by the offer of prizes. It was this journal's prize of £1,000 to the first man to fly across the Channel that was won by Louis Blériot in 1909. The Daily Mail had also offered in November, 1906 a prize of £10,000 to the first person who should fly in twenty-four hours from a place within five miles of their offices in London to the city of Manchester. The distance of such a flight was 183 miles, and as at that time only Wilbur and Orville Wright had had any appreciable success with heavier-than-air machines it was generally regarded as highly improbable that anyone would be able to fly such a distance over all sorts of country, cities, villages, rivers and hills.

It was an expensive business to build airplanes and the opportunity to win such a large prize was very tempting to aviators, but it was some time before anyone was daring enough to try such a long flight. Not until 1910 was an actual attempt made to win the award and the competitor then was Claude Grahame-White. His first flying had been in a Blériot monoplane; later he had bought a Farman biplane, which, although not very fast, was steady and easy to drive. In this machine the pilot sat forward of the lower plane and in front of him was an elevating plane that was used in conjunction with a similar plane at the rear. Grahame-White decided to try for the Daily Mail's prize in this Farman biplane.

Such was the novelty of aerial adventure in days when airplanes were easily daunted by winds and weather, that a great crowd gathered at a quarter past five on a cold morning, April 23, 1910, to watch Grahame-White make his ascent from a field at Park Royal, near Willesden Junction. The official starting point was the gasometer near Wormwood Scrubs and the aviator rounded this successfully and laid his course above the tracks of the London and North-Western Railway to the town of Rugby. Rugby he reached at 7.20 A. M., having made an unprecedented cross-country journey of 85 miles. The air was so cold that he was almost frozen, but having landed and warmed himself for an hour, he started off again, making for Crewe. The wind was rising and blowing strongly and the engine was not working to the best advantage, so he was forced to descend near Lichfield, about 117 miles from London. The increased freshening of the gale prevented his continuing that day and so spoiled that attempt to win the prize, as the conditions of the award called for the journey to be made within twenty-four hours from the start. The next day the wind turned the machine over and the injuries that it sustained prevented Grahame-White making a second attempt at that time.

The Farman biplane was taken to Wormwood Scrubs for repairs. While it was in the shop another competitor, a Frenchman, Louis Paulhan, appeared on the scene. With two entries for the prize, an Englishman and a Frenchman, public excitement greatly heightened, and throngs visited Grahame-White's headquarters at Wormwood Scrubs and Paulhan's headquarters at Hendon.

Early on April twenty-seventh Paulhan's machine arrived at Hendon and the French aviator unpacked and assembled it. The wind was light at three o'clock in the afternoon and Paulhan decided to start, without making any preliminary spins. He set a message to the official observers, and at 5.30 P.M. set off in his machine, which, like that of his rival, had been built by Henri Farman.

Paulhan's wife, some mechanics and friends, motored from headquarters to Willesden, and there boarded a special train which was to follow the flight, a comparatively easy matter as the aviator would set his route by the rails, which were whitewashed at junctions to guide him. The Frenchman got a good start, but he had to fight against the wind on his way north from London; moreover the weather was very cold. Presently he sighted the special train; the engine blew three blasts from its whistle and a big white signal cloth floated from the window of the rear coach. A pelting rainstorm lashed him for some time when he flew above Rugby. In his own account that was published in the Daily Mail he says: "I flew until it was quite dark. All I could make out beneath me was the smoke of the train once in a while, and an occasional flicker of lights from a village. I came down rapidly from 300 metres to 100, so that I could be more certain of my direction.

"Then came the most exciting incident of my flight. . . . I saw the lights of Lichfield. I decided to alight in some convenient meadow before reaching the town, and to do this I sank down to 150 feet. I was immediately above what looked like a large factory with a chimney. So, to alight safely in the field with no damage done, I made a fishhook turn, and my machine was now pointing towards London.

"Suddenly my motor stopped, every drop of petrol exhausted, and the machine swooped downwards almost like a stone dropping. What should I do? Beneath me was the brewery and a certain smash. Behind me was the narrow field which was almost a spider's web with a mesh of telegraph wires. I had an imperceptible fraction of a second in which to make up my mind, and I decided to risk the telegraph wires. As I sank I made a sharp twist right back on the line of my course, and was lucky enough to lift myself over the wires."

Meanwhile the eager crowds that had collected about Grahame-White's shed at Wormwood Scrubs saw the English aviator tuning up his machine. In the early afternoon he had brought out the biplane and climbed into the pilot's seat; the wind, however, was very gusty and he had decided to wait until weather conditions should be more favorable. People kept flocking to see their English champion start off, but the wind increased and at length Grahame-White determined to postpone the flight until next day. But at 6 P. M. word arrived that Paulhan had started from Hendon. Grahame-White had been taking a nap; now, half-awake, he got his airplane out from its shed and declared he should go at once in pursuit of the Frenchman.

The wind was exceedingly gusty, but at 6.30 P. M. the aviator left the ground and, circling over the official starting mark, set off towards Manchester. The biplane could not make much speed, as it had to contend with a strong breeze, but it reached Bletchley at 7.35 P.M. It was now growing dark and Grahame-White descended in a field near Roade, having made a flight of 60 miles.

Paulhan was 57 miles ahead when the two aviators rested for the night. Grahame-White was a keen sportsman and instead of waiting until daylight he started off again at 2.30 A. M. This was an adventurous proceeding, for ascending in darkness had never been attempted before, but the aviator got his bearings by the glare of the automobile headlights and pointed his biplane towards the lights of the railway station.

"I could see absolutely nothing of the ground below me," Grahame-White related in the Daily Mail. "It was all a black smudge. I went right over the railway station lights and then—fortunately only for a second or so—my engine missed fire. I began to sink towards the inky darkness below me. I could have picked no landing. It would become a swift, steep glide to—I know not what. And then, to my joy, my engine picked up again and I rose once more.

"A great difficulty presented itself in not knowing in the darkness whether I was ascending or not. I had done no night flying before, but I soon became accustomed to watching closely the movements of my elevating plane, which was silhouetted before me against the sky. I steered on for a spell with nothing at all to guide me after leaving the lights of Roade behind. . . . Faint lights shone here and there. Some, no doubt, were cottage windows, others I think were the headlights of motor cars.

"I passed over Weedon, my eyes becoming more accustomed to the darkness. On I flew. The weirdness of the sensation can scarcely be described. I was alone in the darkness, with the roar of my engine in my ears. As I glanced back, small, bright flashes of light—the discharge of the exhaust gases from the motor—flashed out in the night. . . .

"At a little inn by the roadside near the village of Crick my friend Mr. Frederick Coleman had promised to draw up his motor car, shining its headlights upon a wall to act as a guide for me. I was keenly on the lookout for this unmistakable night sign, and, sure enough, I saw it quite distinctly below me soon after I had left Welton Station behind. I deviated a little from my course and headed for this patch of light. I saw the motor-car moving as I approached; then, with its headlights throwing a great path of light down the roadway, it set off at a breakneck pace, its driver evidently meaning to guide me on my way. Leaving the railway line on my left, I followed the light on the motor-car, and for a mile or so I hovered almost directly above it, allowing it to act as my pilot.

"But while I was doing so I chanced to glance over to the left again. Coming down the railway line I espied a goods train: it was making for Rugby. 'This,' I thought, 'will be a splendid guide,' and so I swung away from the lights of the motor-car and flew off till I was over the train.

"I saw the lights of Rugby, flew over the town, and forged ahead. The daylight began to come now, and from here on to the point of my descent in a field near Polesworth, my struggle was not with the darkness but with the wind. It was fierce gusts which eventually brought me down."

Grahame-White alighted near Polesworth at 4.14 A. M. and was only a few miles from Paulhan, who did not ascend from Lichfield until 4.09 A. M. The Frenchman flew north, following the route of the railway tracks, over which the special train was keeping pace with him. Everywhere there were crowds, greeting the man in the sky. Cheers rose from throngs at Stafford and Crewe. Didsbury, a southern suburb of Manchester, was the goal of the flight, and there thousands had gathered to see the end of the contest between the Englishman and the Frenchman. The news of Grahame-White's daring night flight had been telegraphed and it was thought that he might yet overtake Paulhan. The wires told that the Frenchman had left Lichfield, but there was no news of the English aviator. Then a biplane was seen winging up from the horizon, and into Didsbury pulled the special train that was pacing Paulhan. The crowds gave a roar of cheers for the Frenchman, who curved above them in the air and brought his machine to the ground at 5.32 A. M. He had made the 183 miles in 242 minutes of actual flying and had won the Daily Mail's prize.

Blériot's air-voyage across the Channel and Paulhan's successful flight from London to Manchester roused tremendous interest in aviation. In the United States the Wright brothers were winning many honors, and Glenn H. Curtiss was supplementing their work with inventions of his own. Curtiss, an inventor and manufacturer of motorcycles and a champion motorcycle rider, set to work to build airplanes along novel lines and presently constructed a biplane that was driven by one high-speed propeller. As the method of obtaining stability by the warping of the wings, according to the Wrights' inven-

Henri Farman, One of Aviation's Great Pioneers,
Flying in 1908

The Wright Brothers' First Hydroplane

tion, was patented, he used little hinged planes, known as ailerons, which were placed at the extremities of the upper wing. In a machine of this type he made many record flights. In July, 1908 Curtiss won the prize offered by the Scientific American by making a flight of over a mile, and the following year he captured the James Gordon Bennett prize in France for attaining the greatest speed. He also made a flight from Albany to Governor's Island, a distance of 142 miles, at an average rate of about 49 miles an hour, with three stops to replenish oil and gasoline.

As a result of these achievements the Curtiss biplane became a popular type and machines made on his designs were manufactured on a large scale. In 1910 Curtiss enlarged the field of use of the airplane by devising the first commercialized hydroplane, a most important step in the history of aviation over wide stretches of water.

CHAPTER VIII

ATTEMPTING THE ATLANTIC
BY DIRIGIBLE BALLOON

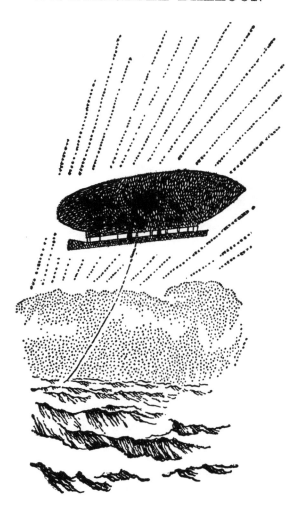

VIII

ATTEMPTING THE ATLANTIC BY DIRIGIBLE BALLOON

TO fly across the Atlantic Ocean had long been a dream of aviators, but it was not until 1910 that the first actual attempt was made to voyage through the air across that vast stretch of water. The daring aerial navigator was Walter Wellman, an American, who proposed to make the journey from the United States to Europe in a dirigible balloon.

Wellman had had a great deal of experience in exploration and navigation both on the sea and in the air and had studied assiduously the possibilities of reaching the North Pole by the aerial route. On an exploring expedition in a Norwegian ice-steamer in 1894 he had been shipwrecked in Spitzbergen and the difficulties of pushing on to the Pole by vessel and dog-sledge had shown him the great advantages of voyaging by aircraft. He made another Arctic expedition by steamer a few years later, spent a winter in Franz Josef Land, and set out on a dash for the Pole in the spring. A gigantic iceberg that crashed through the ice-sheet blocked the road and the little party was forced to retreat. Then Wellman decided to see if some better means than the prim-

itive dog-sledge could not be found for the attempt
to reach the Pole.

His attention had already been drawn to the
practical success of the dirigible balloon in France,
where the government had adopted it as a military
machine. If it was serviceable for war, why might
it not be equally valuable for geographic exploration? Going to Paris in 1906, he investigated the
various types of dirigibles and gave an order for
an airship. This dirigible—christened the *America*
—was 185 feet long, had a volume of 258,500 cubic
feet, and an engine of 70–80 horsepower. She was
ready to start from Camp Wellman in Spitzbergen
in the summer of 1907, and had aboard ten sledge-
dogs, sledges, a small boat, all the accoutrements
for a sledging party, provisions for the crew for
ten months, repair outfit, 250 pounds of lubricant,
300 pounds of fresh water, and 5,750 pounds of gasoline for the engine.

Before starting Wellman wrote this memorandum
of the plan of the voyage:

"To achieve success it is only necessary for the
America to carry us somewhere near to the Pole,
because, as already explained, we go prepared to do
the remainder of the work and the return journey
by sledging. The *America* can proceed with her engines for 120 hours at a rate of 18 miles per hour.
The average wind of the polar ocean in July and
August is 10 miles an hour. If we were so unfortu-

nate as to have a wind of average force blowing
directly contrary to our course throughout the whole
time, we could still make headway at the rate of
eight miles per hour for 120 hours, or a total of 960
miles. The distance from our headquarters to the
Pole is 717 miles (statute).

"Assuming the Pole once attained, and the fuel
supply exhausted, there is every reason to believe
the *America* could remain in the air, using her equilibrator several days longer; and in that time there
is a large chance that the winds would carry her as
a free or drifting balloon far toward, or perhaps to,
some land, and any land would mean safety for the
crew.

"Should this alternative fail, we have not put all
our eggs in one basket, nor in two baskets, for there
is the third recourse, already spoken of—sledging
our way out; and, as shown, we go prepared not only
for the summer and autumn, but with provisions
enough to enable us to remain out, in case of need,
the entire winter, sledging back the following spring,
which is the most favorable season for Arctic
travel."

Stormy weather delayed the making of a trial
trip in the *America* until September, but on the
second day of that month the dirigible was brought
from the balloon house and set free. The engine
started, and the crew of three were off on their
voyage; it was too late in the season for a propitious

attack on the Pole, yet Wellman and his two mates were determined to attempt it if the ship worked right.

Over the mountainous coast they sailed and the open Arctic Ocean was before them. Wellman gave the order to the man at the wheel: "Head her north!" North went the dirigible until she ran into a snowstorm that threatened to beat her down on a lee coast. Three times she was almost wrecked on precipitious cliffs, but each time the motor and pro-peller brought her away safely.

Wellman saw that the only thing to do was to try to land the airship where she could be saved. This was no easy task in such a storm as was raging, but presently he let out some of the gas and brought the dirigible down on the surface of a glacier. The cloth of the deflated balloon lay across two crevasses, but the mechanism was intact. After a few hours two steamers that had been on the lookout rescued the crew and the airship and took them back to head-quarters.

Winter was now setting in and the *America* was returned to Paris to be overhauled. It was two years later when Wellman, on August 15, 1909, with three companions started from Spitzbergen again in the *America* over the polar sea. This time the weather was fine and the airship sailed along at a rate close to twenty-five knots an hour, which the navigators estimated would bring them to the Pole in less than thirty hours. Then something happened—the equilibrator broke loose, and down into the ocean went 1,200 pounds of the balancing device and its contents of reserve provisions.

Without the equilibrator the dirigible would soon become unmanageable. They must turn back to Spitzbergen. A retarder or drag-anchor was dropped and the airship was brought about. Fortunately a Norwegian government vessel came that way and towed her back to camp, which she reached after having voyaged 120 miles.

Meantime Commander Peary had reached the North Pole and Wellman, considering that great quest of explorers completed, commenced making plans for another project that had long been in his mind, the attempt to cross the Atlantic Ocean by dirigible balloon.

The *America,* in which he planned to travel, had already been twice tested in flights of considerable length over northern seas and had been reconstructed since her second voyage. The balloon was of a non-rigid type, and in its improved form measured 228 feet in length, had a capacity of 350,000 cubic feet, and a lifting power of about six tons. The balloon reservoir was composed of cotton, silk and rubber; the silk and cotton gave great strength to resist the outward pressure of the gas, the rubber held the gas with a small percentage of leakage. Underneath the balloon proper was a long, enclosed car, in shape something like a gangway. There was also a detachable lifeboat. The propulsive power was provided by two motors, capable of making a speed of twenty miles an hour.

The peculiar feature of Wellman's airship was the equilibrator, which was like a large guide rope, intended to trail on the surface of the water and keep the dirigible automatically at the proper height, thereby dispensing with the need of letting out gas or throwing out ballast. Through the centre of it ran a cable made of steel, more than 100 yards in length, and fastened at one end to the airship. To this cable were tied a number of cylindrical wooden blocks, connected by ball-and-socket joints; at the upper part there was a series of gasoline tanks, shaped like the wooden blocks, and these could be drawn up to the car as circumstances dictated. Wellman considered this equilibrator of great importance to a successful flight.

Aboard the airship was a wireless receiving and transmitting installation, which might prove of invaluable service on such an unprecedented voyage. It was 3500 miles from America to Europe and the longest airship voyage that had been made up to that time was only about 900 miles, and that over land. The plan was to follow as closely as possible the steamship route from New York to the English Channel.

At eight o'clock in the morning on October 15, 1910 the airship *America* started from Atlantic City. Wellman was in command, Murray Simon was navigator, Melvin Vaniman chief engineer, Jack Irwin wireless operator. In addition there were two assistant engineers, Loud and Aubert, which made up a crew of six.

As mascot there was a small gray cat, and this feline passenger provided the first adventure of the voyage; a motor boat towed the dirigible some distance out to sea, then the airship's motors started and the trip began, whereupon the cat commenced to howl. Puss was put in a bag and Vaniman tried to lower him to the motor boat, but this had now cast off the tow line and puss was hauled up again. Fed on biscuits, the little passenger quickly accommodated himself to travel through the air.

The *America* moved smoothly out over the Atlantic; there was a light breeze from the northwest; down below through the fog the mariners could see the equilibrator swimming like a sea serpent, its head in the air, and making a curving, foamy wake. All the mechanism was working well and the fog, which continued thick for sometime after starting, proved no hindrance to progress. After voyaging for two hours and a half the motor was stopped in order to try the wireless. Jack Irwin picked up a message in the air from Atlantic City:

"Wellman, Airship *America*:
    We are getting your signals. What news?"

To this the commander sent this reply:

"Headed northeast. All well on board. Machinery working well. Good-bye,

Wellman."

Those were the first wireless messages ever exchanged between a station on shore and an airship navigating the ocean.

Other messages were sent back and forth. Presently one of the motors had to be stopped, as sand in the bearings was making it run hot. While it was being cleaned the airship drifted northwards. The motor worked satisfactorily for an hour, then had to be stopped and cleaned again. These delays were a great annoyance, for the sea was quiet and the wind was blowing in the right direction. In his account Wellman said: "This day was virtually wasted. By nightfall, nearly ten hours out, we were sighted and reported by the steamer *Coamo,* about eighty miles from Atlantic City, when we should have been two hundred."

There were other difficulties to contend with. In the afternoon the dirigible rose 100 feet above the sea, which lifted thirteen tanks of the equilibrator above the water. Now the equilibrator began to be a nuisance, its drag became a series of jerks instead of a steady pull, which hindered forward movement and caused discomfort to the crew. As night came on the gas in the balloon contracted and some of the precious gasoline which should have been used in the engine had to be thrown overboard to make up for the loss of buoyancy. The exhaust pipe heated red hot and began to send out sparks, which threatened to set fire to the canvas and blow up the whole ship.

At eight that night the *America* almost ran into a schooner; fortunately the lookout sighted the ship and gave the warning in time for the steersman to throw the helm hard to starboard and so avoid a collision. At the same time a fresh breeze sprang up from the south-southwest and blew the airship towards the coast of New England instead of east on the sea.

Next morning the *America* was over Martha's Vineyard, between Nantucket lightship and the mainland, some 250 miles northeast of Atlantic City. Early in the day heavy gusts from the southwest blew the airship forward at tremendous speed and caused the submerged equilibrator to pull so hard that it almost brought the *America* down to the water. To lighten the ship more gasoline, a heavy cable and various spare articles were thrown overboard. The motor was stopped and the dirigible drifted 140 miles beyond Nantucket and out towards the transatlantic steamship lanes.

"All through this day," Wellman says of the second day of the voyage, "we wondered if the steel car could withstand the strains put upon it by the equilibrator cables as the steel serpent jumped from wave to wave, fifty to eighty feet each leap." The outlook was gloomy, and when late in the afternoon the wind slackened somewhat and the sea was not so rough the navigators considered launching the lifeboat and leaving the dirigible; it was decided, however, to stick by the ship.

So they kept on, snatching a little sleep now and then, munching cold meat and ship biscuits; that Sunday evening they started up the gasoline stove in the lifeboat, fried bacon and eggs and boiled coffee and had a royal feast. The equilibrator was now more than ever a handicap, its weight, floating on the waves, kept dragging the airship down. More gasoline had to be thrown out to prevent the lifeboat from being torn away as it struck the water. The larger motor had to be dumped over, and now with the motor lost and most of the gasoline and with the wind strong in the northeast the question was how to save the company aboard from destruction in the sea.

At noon on Monday they took a reckoning from the sun and figured that they were about four hundred miles east of Hampton Roads. They decided on this plan: to keep the one motor they had and all the gasoline they could, in reserve for a final effort to reach the Bermudas or the coast of Florida, and meanwhile to allow the airship to drift with the wind.

The problem of how to get themselves out of the airship and safely into the lifeboat on the sea was one that they studied carefully. Wellman says: "The

America was running an average of from 15 to 18 knots per hour with the wind. She was drifting broadside of the course, which meant that as the lifeboat was launched into the sea, it, too, must take the water headside on. What we asked ourselves, over and over, was this: Will not the craft be instantly capsized and foundered? And if she be lucky enough to escape that fate, how about the equilibrator, tearing along a few feet in the rear? Will it not strike the struggling boat with the force of its two-tons moving rapidly through the water, act as a battering ram, and smash us to pieces?"

That Monday afternoon there was doubt whether they could keep the airship afloat, as the gas cooled after the sun set. Fortunately the night was warm, the gas did not contract very much, and only a little lubricant and some parts of the motor had to be thrown overboard. A full moon in a cloudless sky illuminated the ocean. The crew took turns at sleeping and those on watch searched the horizon for steamer or sail.

Early on Tuesday morning Wellman thought he saw the lights of a ship. Irwin tried his wireless, but got no response; then with his electric "blinker" he sent light signals by the Morse code. The ship answered the signals; she was a steamer from Bermuda, the *Trent*. The steamer headed for the airship and Wellman's party made ready to launch the lifeboat. This proved very difficult, and while they were attempting it the dirigible lost her equilibrium and almost capsized, end over end. When they had brought her on an even keel again the gas cord was pulled, which let out hydrogen, and the airship began to descend to the water. The crew—and the small gray cat, the faithful mascot,—took their places in the lifeboat.

When the boat was only four or five feet above the water the two release-hooks were let go, and up went the lightened airship and down went the boat. The boat almost capsized, but righted herself; then the equilibrator hit the boat, stove a hole in the forward compartment and bruised two of the crew. By this time the *Trent* was bearing down as if to smash the cockleshell craft; the steamer's prow hit the boat a glancing blow, the little boat sheered off and ran along the big ship's port quarter. A line was thrown out and caught. The lifeboat was borne along to the whirlpool of the steamer's propellers, rocked, pitched and righted again—the crew scrambled up to safety. "That must have been our ninth escape from Davy Jones' locker," said Murray Simon the navigator; "told you it was a good thing to have a cat along—cats have nine lives!"

Away the *America* floated and disappeared from sight, after having carried Wellman and his mates a little more than a thousand miles over the sea.

That was the end of the voyage, which had lasted almost three days. Wellman afterwards admitted that all chances of crossing the Atlantic were wrecked by the equilibrator, which placed a terrific strain on the structure of the airship, as well as made the position of the crew much more difficult by its constant jerks and gyrations in air and water. Except for the equilibrator the *America* was a success; the balloon held the gas well and the motors were effective as soon as the trouble with the bearings had been corrected. Wellman's daring attempt made it appear possible that an airship would some day voyage from America to Europe.

CHAPTER IX

THE ZEPPELINS

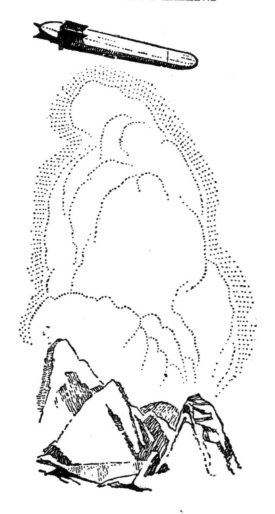

IX

THE ZEPPELINS

THE dirigible balloons constructed by Santos-Dumont were of the non-rigid type, or, in other words, depended entirely on being kept inflated in order to maintain their shape. While Santos-Dumont was experimenting in Paris a German inventor, Count Ferdinand von Zeppelin, was working on a different type of dirigible balloon, a "rigid" airship, in which the shape was maintained by the use of a rigid, fabric-covered frame, and the gas was stored in separate compartments.

Zeppelin retired from the German Army in 1891, and having been an enthusiastic student of aeronautics he set to work to produce what he considered would be a practicable airship. The non-rigid balloon with the single chamber for gas he thought both insecure and inefficient; what he wanted was an airship that would not change its shape and would obtain its buoyancy from a number of independent gas-containers that did not need to be kept taut. If the airship could maintain its shape under all conditions it could be more easily propelled, while if the gas were in a number of bags the deflation of any one would not destroy the balloon's buoyancy; thus the airship would gain greatly in practical control and in safety.

His plan was to construct a rigid framework covered with fabric and to use aluminum alloy in building the framework, which would give great strength relative to its weight. The weight of an airship built on his plan would be heavier than that of a nonrigid one, and therefore it seemed to him that the rigid airship should be very large, since the weight of the framework would constitute a smaller proportion of the total weight the larger the airship were built.

The dirigible of his invention was to be much more like an aerial ship than the balloons of Santos-Dumont were; the rigid hull could be made with a tapering stern, which would increase speed, the engines and propellers, placed close to the hull, could exert their force near the centre of the airship, the rudders could be turned easily without affecting the stability of the balloon. Having experimented for some time and assured himself of the practicability of his invention, Zeppelin applied to the German Government for financial assistance to enable him to carry on his work on a large scale. The government was not interested in what they considered a visionary scheme, and therefore Zeppelin organized a stock company with a capital of 800,000 marks.

His next step was to employ two engineers to work on his designs and then to build an airship shed, which he moored near Friedrichshafen, on Lake

Constance. This shed floated on the water and the central part of the floor was made in the form of a pontoon, which could be brought out from the structure with the airship on it. The first dirigible he built—the first rigid airship ever constructed—consisted of a row of seventeen balloons confined in a cylindrical shell 416 feet long and 38 feet in diameter, with pointed ends. This could be driven forward or backward by screw propellers attached to cars underneath and the steering was done by two rudders, one placed forward and one aft. The propellers were worked by two Daimler benzine engines, each of 16 horsepower.

In July, 1900, Count Zeppelin made his first trial trip in this airship, the LZ 1, over Lake Constance. The airship steered admirably both vertically and horizontally, its best speed was about 8½ miles an hour. In handling it, however, the LZ 1 was somewhat damaged and had to be kept in dock some months for repairs.

The next October the LZ 1 made another trip and attained a speed of 17 miles an hour, the greatest speed yet achieved by an airship. Zeppelin was hailed as a hero and acclaimed throughout Germany as the first man to invent a ship that would ride successfully through the air. He wanted to build a new dirigible to an improved design, but the stock company's funds were now depleted. An appeal to the public, however, brought in sufficient money to allow him to construct the LZ 2.

This second Zeppelin airship was shorter than the first one, but it was propelled by two 85 horsepower motors. It made several successful voyages; then, on one of its flights, there was trouble with the engines and steering gear and it made a forced descent in a meadow. It alighted without harm, but a strong wind rose and wrecked the LZ 2 in a few minutes.

Count Zeppelin now considered giving up aeronautics, but the urge to persevere was strong, and within nine months he built the LZ 3. This dirigible was so successful that it was used as a model for other airships and the German Government bought it and assigned it to the army as the first unit of an aerial fleet. The government also made the inventor a grant of money, with which he constructed the LZ 4, larger than the others and with two 110 horsepower motors, each of which drove three propellers. This the government agreed to buy if it could fly for twenty-four hours without alighting and could land and rise again without outside aid. On July 1, 1908, the LZ 4 made the longest voyage yet attained by a dirigible balloon, and on August fourth Count Zeppelin was ready for the government trial trip.

The airship left Friedrichshafen at 6.02 A. M. and, following the line of the Rhine, journeyed through the air over Basle, Colmar, Strasburg, Carlsruhe and Mannheim, to Mayence, which she reached at 6 P. M. Here she waited several hours to repair one of the motors. She had made an out-

bound journey of about 300 miles, and at 11 P. M.
set off southward to return to Friedrichshafen. On
this trip the loss of gas forced the airship to descend at 8 A. M. the next morning at Echterdingen,
440 miles from the start of the return voyage. Gas
cylinders were secured to inflate the gas bags, but
while the work was being done a squall commenced
to buffet the balloon. Two of the engineers sprang
into one of the dirigible's cars and started the motor, but the wind sent the balloon bumping and
bounding along the ground; then one of the gasoline
tanks burst and immediately the LZ 4 was wrapped
in flames.

Great was the sympathy of all Germany for Count
Zeppelin in this catastrophe, and a large Zeppelin
fund was at once subscribed by people throughout
the nation, augmented by a grant from the government. The Count was now more of a popular hero
than ever and he was assured of plenty of money
with which to continue his work. He built a new
dirigible, and in June, 1909 set out from Lake Constance with the plan of flying, if possible, to Berlin,
as the people of the capital had not yet seen a Zeppelin.

Late on a Saturday evening the great airship
started on her journey, flew steadily north all night
and most of the next day and at 7.10 P. M. on Sunday reached Bitterfield, some 70 miles from Berlin.
Passing above Leipzig Count Zeppelin had dropped
a telegram addressed to the airship battalion at Ber-

lin, in which he requested assistance if he should land there. The Kaiser was informed of the message and at once he ordered a mobilisation of all the near-by troops in the Templehof Field. This would give the Count a magnificent welcome and furnish the people with a dramatic setting for the arrival of the Zeppelin.

The troops and the enthusiastic Berliners waited on the field for hours; then came word that a shortage of gasoline had compelled the airship to turn south. Sunday night it sailed smoothly above the Thuringian Forest and the Swabian Alps and on Monday morning was cheered by the people of Stuttgart as it made a circle around the palace of the Crown Prince of Wurtemberg. From there it went on to Goppingen, less than 50 miles from Friedrichshafen, where it attempted to descend in order to replenish the fuel. As it settled close to the ground, however, a gust of wind blew it against a tree and it was so much damaged that it had to be laid up several weeks for repairs. Notwithstanding this mishap the voyage had been a remarkable one and set a new record, much surpassing all previous flights; the Zeppelin had flown almost 1000 miles in a continuous journey of 38 hours.

Count Zeppelin built his first passenger airship, the *Deutschland,* in 1910. This dirigible had three motors, of 120 horsepower each, and was furnished with a luxurious central cabin and a restaurant. It made many successful trips and delighted German travellers with the novel experience of gliding smoothly through the air. On a June morning it started out from Düsseldorf with 23 passengers to make a round trip of several hours. The wind began to rise and one of the motors got out of order, so, as it would have been a risky business to turn and try to run with the wind, the pilot attempted to drive the dirigible against the gale to Münster, where there was a suitable place for landing. The two engines that were working were unable to make headway and for a considerable time the *Deutschland* floundered in the air, tossing up and down. Rain, beating heavily, obscured the view. There was likely to be a disaster unless the situation improved before the supply of gasoline was used up.

The gasoline tanks ran dry and the motors ceased turning; then the storm picked up the airship and hurled it into a forest, where it crashed against the trees. The Zeppelin was wrecked, but fortunately all those on board were able to reach the ground by a rope ladder and escaped unhurt.

Notwithstanding this misadventure and many others, Count Zeppelin kept on building his dirigibles for passenger service and military and naval use. He had constructed twenty-six by 1914, and was able to drive his airships at a speed of 50 miles an hour. Meanwhile the German Air Travel Company had been organized and was utilizing Zeppelins for passenger journeys. In three years of service the four airships *Schwaben, Viktoria Luise, Hansa,* and

Sachsen made 760 flights and carried 14,000 passengers; the distance they covered totalled almost 100,-000 miles. In all these flights there was not one mishap, nor was any passenger injured.

Zeppelin's rigid airships had proved their superiority for long voyages over all other types of airships or airplanes and had demonstrated that transport through the air was a practical proposition and might be made as serviceable as transport by seagoing ships or land-going railroads. In carrying capacity the rigid airship is unrivalled, and its steadiness and economy give it a great advantage in long, non-stop journeys. Many remarkable flights have been made by this type of airship.

A Zeppelin set out from Jamboli, in Bulgaria, on November 21, 1917, to carry more than 20 tons of medical supplies to the German forces that were fighting the British in German East Africa. The dirigible flew across the Mediterranean and followed the Nile as far as Khartoum. When she was above the Victoria Nyanza she picked up a wireless message from Germany, which stated that the place where she had been intending to land had been captured by the British and ordered her to return to Bulgaria. Thereupon the Zeppelin turned and, flying back over her former route, reached Jamboli exactly four days after she had started from there; she had accomplished a non-stop voyage of 5,500 miles and had travelled at an average speed of 57 miles an hour.

Another remarkable flight was that of the ZR 3, which left Friedrichshafen in November of 1924, crossed France and Spain, and proceeded direct for New York, with good weather to aid her. When above the Gulf Stream the dirigible met high winds but wireless weather reports enabled her to avoid the worst of the storm and, passing over the fog-bound Newfoundland Banks, she turned south and landed on Long Island, having taken just 70 hours to cross the Atlantic, from the mouth of the Gironde River to Sandy Hook.

Such exploits have amply justified Count Ferdinand von Zeppelin's belief in the practical advantages of the rigid airship.

CHAPTER X

AIRCRAFT IN THE WAR

X

AIRCRAFT IN THE WAR

WITH the Great War of 1914–1918 a new element, the airship, entered into the field of combat and strategy. For centuries infantry, cavalry, artillery and warships had dominated the military conflicts of nations; now came a new arrival that revolutionized old ideas and presented unique and amazing possibilities.

In a sense the airship had restored the opportunity for individual achievement that existed in the days of single combat between swordsman and swordsman, knight and knight. Warfare had become largely a matter of cumbersomely moving masses, whether of men or ships. In the air, however, the man of the air relied on his own initiative and planned his own campaign. The opportunity for single-handed adventure had the lure that once appealed to a Roland or Oliver.

The airplane had been very little used in fighting before 1914, practically only in the warfare in the Balkans in 1912. When the Great War began there were very few airplanes equipped with machine-guns and aircraft were considered essentially valuable as scouts, to spy out the movements of the enemy's forces and bring back information to their own headquarters. In this work—as in many other military departments—Germany had the advantage at the start, being possessed of more machines and more experienced pilots than any other nation. The German aviator, Lieutenant Immelman, flew over Paris daily during September, 1914, dropping bombs on the city and a bag of sand, in which was this note:

"People of Paris! Surrender! The Germans are at your gates! To-morrow you will be ours!

Lieutenant Immelmann,
Air Scout."

The bombs he dropped were light and did comparatively little damage, and Paris was soon efficiently protected from airplanes and Zeppelins. Observation towers and listening towers, searchlights and field guns were the city's anti-aircraft land defenses while in the air there was an airplane patrol maintained at three different altitudes, approximately at 1,000, 6,000 and 10,000 feet.

England began the war with some 100 machines and these, together with the more numerous planes of her ally, France, did invaluable service in reporting on the size of the German armies that were pressing through Luxemburg and Belgium; without these scouts the defensive plan of compaign would probably have been very different and the Germans, surprising the Allies by the immensity of their manpower, might well have won the war in a few months.

This first effective use of aircraft from a military

stand-point quickly led to great improvement in the equipping of machines. At first the pilots carried only a revolver or rifle, and perhaps a few bombs. Then machine-guns were placed in the planes and these, by the rapidity of their fire, made up for the difficulty of taking accurate aim from a moving platform at a speeding enemy. The work of aircraft was next divided into three classes, that of the fighting scout, the observation airplane and the bombing machine.

The fighting scout was a one-man machine, small, and with a powerful engine, so that it could travel at rates of speed up to 140 miles an hour, dive, climb, and maneuver with the utmost nimbleness. Such a plane usually carried two machine-guns, one stationed directly in front of the pilot and the other in front and above him. The duties of the fighting scout were varied: to clear the air of enemy machines by chasing and attacking them, to escort the larger and slower observation and bombing machines and protect them from the adversary's scouts, to fly low and attack troops, trains and road convoys, to drive off night raiders, enemy planes and airships, and to set fire to enemy kite-balloons.

The observation airplanes were generally two-seaters and carried an observer in addition to the pilot. The observer was in charge of a Lewis machine-gun that was mounted on a rotating frame that allowed it to cover a wide field of fire, the pilot had another machine-gun fixed in front of his seat as in the fighting scout. These observation planes usually did not fly as high as the scouts; their duty was to search for the enemy troops and direct the gunfire of their own artillery by signaling with colored lights or by wireless. The observer would make notes of the movements of the troops, the positions of the enemy's trenches and artillery, and so supply information to his army headquarters. By the use of specially constructed cameras the observers were able to furnish immensely valuable aerial maps.

The bombing machines were the most powerful planes and carried in addition to a large stock of explosives, fuel for making long trips. They were two-seaters and could fly at heights up to four miles; some of them—the Handley-Pages, for example— had two engines, and could make a journey of 250 miles outward bound and as many more back to their point of starting.

Every movement of troops, guns or supplies was watched from the air, and in consequence "camouflage"—the ingenious disguising of objects in various ways—was raised to a fine art. Before an army set forward swarms of aircraft were sent above the enemy's lines to clear the air of planes and to act as eyes for headquarters. A battle was not, as formerly, fought over so many miles of ground only, but included the air to a height of three or four miles, and the success of the scouts, wheeling about high above the ground, was a very important factor in the success of the infantry and artillery.

The great value of aircraft was strikingly shown in the final campaign of the English against the Turks in Palestine. Before launching their ground attack the English sent their machines far to the rear of the Turkish trenches, where the aviators bombed the enemy airplanes and prevented any of the Turkish machines rising. The Turks therefore had no air scouts to report on the English movements while the English knew exactly what their opponents were doing. When the Turkish troops finally turned and fled, the English airplanes, with no opposition in the sky, routed them completely.

The seaplane, which is similar to the land machine but with large floats in the place of wheels,—picturesquely described as a land machine wearing a pair of big galoshes,—played a large part in the war. It could land on the water, be repaired, and rise into the air again. The Germans used a great many of them to patrol the Baltic, the Heligoland Bight, and the coasts of Holland and Belgium. German seaplanes ordinarily kept on the eastern side of the North Sea, but from there they could threaten the English fleets at Scapa Flow, in the Orkneys, and at Rosyth, in the Firth of Forth, as they might fly above the warships and drop torpedoes among them. To guard against this the English had to employ a large army of rival seaplanes.

The German warships kept in port most of the time and there were no German merchant vessels on the seas, but the English had ships in almost all waters, and as these might be attacked by enemy submarines anywhere the English had to develop aircraft that would be more weatherly and fly longer distances than the seaplane. Such craft were needed to protect the ships from the submarines, and for this purpose the English Admiralty constructed the flying-boat. This had a mahogany hull with hydroplane steps on the bottom which enabled it to rise in the water as it gained speed and acquire sufficient velocity to ascend from the surface by the lifting power of its wings. These flying-boats could travel great distances and successfully ride out all sorts of rough weather.

The English flying-boats carried two pilots, a wireless operator and an engineer, in addition to a full supply of bombs and fuel sufficient for a voyage of seven hours. The German submarines usually traversed the North Sea to the Straits of Dover in order to reach the English Channel and it was in this area that the flying-boats hunted for the undersea craft and when they located one aimed their bombs at it. Besides hunting for submarines the flying-boats were used to convoy the fleets of cargo boats that moved between England and the continent and made long-distance reconnaissance trips to the Heligoland Bight to see what the German ships were doing. By the end of the war some enormous flying-boats had been built. One, called the Porte "Baby," weighed over 15 tons and carried a small airplane. It was propelled by five engines, that totaled 1,800 horsepower, and on a trial trip it took a load of 24 men, seven hours' fuel, and two tons of sand.

The Germans made great use of their Zeppelin airships for patrol service and for night raids over enemy towns. On the English side the most popular airship was the small non-rigid sea scout, jocularly called the "Blimp." This was a combination of a gas envelope and an airplane body, and carried a crew of a pilot, an engineer and a wireless operator. These did splendid work patrolling the coasts, hunting for submarines and locating mines, and furnished invaluable information to the Admiralty concerning all shipping in the areas they covered.

The Zeppelins were constantly used by the Germans during the war. When the German armies invaded Belgium in the first weeks of the conflict Zeppelins accompanied the troops and dropped bombs on Belgian towns. Their speed of movement, great carrying capacity and large radius of action made them more serviceable than any other type of aircraft for raiding England, situated hundreds of miles from their base. On a clear night they could sail across the North Sea at a great height, drop their explosives on English soil, and be off again. The first Zeppelin raid took place on January 19, 1915, and from then on for two years and a half the great German dirigibles attacked English towns and cities, making London their particular target. They ran little risk at first, but when the English organized their anti-aircraft defences the tables were turned; the Zeppelins were forced to fly higher and higher to avoid the searchlights that illuminated them and drew the fire of field guns and English planes. Airplanes hunted the Zeppelins and many of the small craft succeeded in bringing down their gigantic opponents in a blaze of fire. Raiding became more and more hazardous, and eventually the dirigibles had to fly so high that the cold made the engines freeze if they stopped. Several Zeppelins were rendered useless by being frozen up and thereafter the Germans came to rely on their "Gotha" and "Giant" bombing airplanes for raids over enemy country.

The aviators themselves were a wonderful type of men, perhaps the most daring of all adventurers. Maneuvers that in peace times would have been considered foolhardy—looping the loop, side-slipping, rolling, and so forth—became part of the every day flying of the war time pilot. The great pioneer air fighter was the Frenchman, Roland Garros. Before the war he had won renown as an aviator; he was the first to fly over the Mediterranean Sea and captured prizes in air races from Paris to Rome and from Paris to Madrid. When the war began he set to work to invent a method by which he might mount a machine gun on an airplane in such a fashion that the bullets would not hit the propeller. By February, 1915, he had hit upon the device he wanted and was able to send a stream of bullets from the nose of his plane without damage to the machine. In eighteen days he shot down five German planes. On April nineteenth he flew over an enemy supply train that was entering Courtrai, dropped his bombs, and descended to watch the effect of the explosions. He then turned his machine towards home, but to his dismay the engine did not pick up. Something had happened and he came to the ground in the midst of his enemies. He tried to fire his machine, but before he could do this the Germans extinguished the flames and so his invention was at once discovered and straightway copied by his opponents. Thereafter for the greater part of the war Garros was a prisoner. In January, 1918, he escaped from Germany and again entered the air service of France.

At the head of the list of French Aces—to use the name given to the more celebrated of the military aviators—was René Fonck, who was reputed to have been victorious over 126 enemy machines and who was officially credited with 75 victories. The record of his achievements as an aerial duelist is marvelous; he would engage an adversary under almost any conditions. In eight days during his first service in a fighting escadrille he won three victories. On October 21, 1917, he was named a Chevalier of the Legion of Honor with this citation:

"Fighting pilot of great value, uniting with illustrious bravery exceptional qualities of skill and coolness. Entering the fighting escadrille after 500 hours flying in the army corps he has become in a short time one of the best fighting pilots in the French

Army. Brought down his 8th, 9th, and 10th enemy airplanes on August 20th and 21st, 1917. Already cited seven times and holds the Military Medal.''

On May 8, 1918, Fonck brought down three enemy planes with a total of twenty-six shots, and that same afternoon accounted for three more with thirty bullets. In September he flew one day to his customary height of 20,000 feet above the German lines near Montdidier and brought down six enemy planes within two hours. In all this fighting, moreover, no enemy ever succeeded in wounding him nor even in hitting any part of his machine. His skill in maneuvering and outguessing an adversary was miraculous and he is generally considered the greatest of all air fighters.

Most audacious of the French Aces was Georges Guynemer, who was eight times shot down from on high and who time and again escaped destruction by enemy fire only by the smallest chance. On the day he was made an officer of the Legion of Honor he went on a hunt for German planes and had two encounters. When he returned General d'Esperey asked Guynemer to show him his machine. Across the floor of the fuselage on which the aviator's feet rested while they touched the rudder bar there was a row of bullet holes that had been made that morning.

General d'Esperey pointed to them and asked: ''How was it that your feet were not struck?''

During the World War the airplane was developed as a new
instrument of warfare and the first airplane
combats took place

"I had just moved them, my General," was Guynemer's simple answer.

The escadrille to which Guynemer was attached was the Cigognes, which became the greatest fighting squadron in France. During the campaign around Verdun the Cicognes were constantly in the air and none of them more constantly than Guynemer. He flew in all kinds of weather, fought from six to ten combats a day, and returned to the airdrome with his plane a veritable sieve, the wings torn to pieces by shrapnel from anti-aircraft guns.

Guynemer was officially credited with 53 victories, that is victories attested to by three or more eye-witnesses; he probably brought down twice as many enemy planes. On September 11, 1917 he went in pursuit of a German machine and disappeared, leaving no clue as to what had happened to him.

There were many aviators celebrated for exceptional daring and resourcefulness among the flying corps of the various nations engaged in the war. Among the great English Aces was Albert Ball, a most skillful and intrepid fighter who no sooner saw an enemy plane than he darted away to attack it, regardless of whether it was a single machine or part of an opposing formation of ten, fifteen, or twenty adversaries. He received many decorations, among them the Victoria Cross. This is the official citation for one of his many exploits:

"September 16, 1916. Remarkable bravery and skill. Observing a group of seven enemy aeroplanes in battle formation, he attacked one instantly at less than fifteen yards and brought it down. The others took flight. Continuing his patrol he saw five machines; he approached one of them until he was less than ten yards distant and brought it down. He attacked another of them, riddled it with bullets and brought it down. Then he went back to the nearest aerodrome for more ammunition. He set out again, attacked three new enemy aeroplanes and brought them down out of control. Having no more gas he returned with his machine riddled with bullets.''

William A. Bishop, a Canadian, was credited with 72 victories and was decorated with the greatly-prized Victoria Cross. It was his custom to fly over an enemy airdrome and challenge the German champions to come aloft. His Nieuport machine was a faster climber than the enemy Albatross planes and he won many combats by his ability to maneuver at a superior height.

The first American escadrille, known as the Escadrille Lafayette, was made up of William Thaw, Norman Prince, Eliot Cowdin, Bert Hall, Kiffin Yates Rockwell, James McConnell, and Victor Chapman. These aviators won their first honors above the fields of Verdun and from then on achieved great and well-deserved reputations as dashing fighters. Other Americans renowned for their ability as aerial pilots were Edward V. Rickenbacker, who was given the unofficial title of the American Ace of Aces because of his 25 attested victories, and Raoul Lufbery, whose many narrow escapes rivalled those of the French Guynemer.

Great Britain awarded sixteen Victoria Crosses to her airmen. The United States awarded its Medal of Honor to one aviator for his valor in the war, to Frank Luke, Jr., of Phoenix, Arizona. This young aviator was a marvelous airplane fighter, one who achieved almost incredible successes and escapes. He was killed in combat near the village of Murvaux, and the Congress of the United States paid tribute to his memory by the award of the Congressional Medal: "For conspicuous gallantry and intrepidity above and beyond the call of duty."

The Germans had their great aviator-hero, von Richthofen, and every nation in the war its outstanding air champions. Most of them were young, many mere boys. The air gave them the opportunity to attempt more daring adventures than the land and like eagles they flew, circled, and met in combat in the sky.

Roland and Oliver returned in these aviators who soared on mighty wings above the fields of France.

CHAPTER XI

THE AIRPLANE ESSAYS THE ATLANTIC

XI

THE AIRPLANE ESSAYS THE ATLANTIC

WHEN the airplane had justified itself by
such flights as that across the English
Channel and from London to Manchester
those who were interested in aviation began to pon-
der the tempting problem of flying by airplane across
the Atlantic Ocean. The English newspaper, the
Daily Mail, which had already sponsored so many
record-making flights, offered in April, 1913 a prize
of £10,000 to the crew of the first airplane that
should accomplish this new feat. The flight might
be made from any place in the British Isles to any
place in Newfoundland, Canada, or the United States
or might be made in the reverse direction; the trip
must be completed in 72 consecutive hours; machines
were not to be changed during the flight, although
repairs might be made on the journey, and the flight
must be a non-stop one, without descent at the Azores. Under these conditions the flight would have
to cover at least 1,880 miles, which is the distance
from the most western point of Ireland to the coast
of Newfoundland.

This prize aroused great interest in Europe and
America, but the advent of the war caused a suspen-

sion of the Daily Mail's offer, which was, however, renewed after the signing of the Armistice in November, 1918. In the following year a contestant entered the lists, an Australian, Harry Hawker, who was a daring and very accomplished aviator. He had been connected with the Sopwith Aviation Company during the war and this company now offered to build him a special machine for a transatlantic flight, which offer he accepted.

The machine they built, which was named the *Atlantic,* was a biplane with a single 350 horsepower engine, and its total weight at the start, with a crew of two and fuel and water aboard, was about 2¾ tons. The under carriage was detachable and could be dropped when the plane got away from the land, and the upper part of the machine was made like a wooden boat, inverted, which might be very convenient if the biplane were obliged to land in the ocean.

Hawker and his navigator, Lieutenant-Commander Kenneth Mackenzie-Grieve, R.N., tested the *Atlantic* by making a non-stop flight of 1,800 miles at the Brooklands Airdrome. They had decided to try to cross the ocean from west to east and therefore sailed from England aboard ship with their plane and arrived at St. Johns, Newfoundland, in March, 1919.

The plan was to start the flight on or about April sixteenth, a period of full moon, and they figured that if they left Newfoundland at 10 P. M (Greenwich time) they should be able to reach Ireland the next afternoon. It was difficult to find suitable ground for an airdrome near St. Johns, and when a site was finally selected at Mount Pearl Farm the place soon became almost a quagmire from snow and rain. The weather was not favorable for flying, and while Hawker and his companion waited for suitable conditions a rival machine, a Martynside, arrived at St. Johns and the crews of the two machines watched each other like hawks, each wanting to get the first start. On the date set, April sixteenth, there was a snow storm. The inclement weather continued and at the end of a month the aviators and the public were beginning to wonder if the flyers would ever get off.

By the middle of May air conditions were improved and Hawker determined to make a start. Three American flying-boats had left the United States on May sixteenth heading for Europe by way of the Azores and the commander of the *Atlantic* did not want to lose the honor of being first to fly across the ocean. So at 3 P. M. on May eighteenth Hawker and Mackenzie-Grieve donned their flying garb, the outer part of which was a rubber suit with inflatable air-bags which would buoy up the wearers if they should fall into the water. In the top or boat part of the machine they stowed emergency rations, paddles, and colored lights to be used for signaling, and in the main body of the airplane thermos bottles of coffee, sandwiches and foods of various kinds in small, compressed form.

The *Atlantic* rose from its airdrome at 5.51 P. M.

(Greenwich time) and flew down the hill of Mount Pearl Farm. The biplane was heavily loaded with 350 gallons of gasoline and narrowly escaped colliding with a fence; a miss was as good as a mile, however, and it soared aloft above the suburbs of St. Johns, and from the air Hawker saw the rival Martynside plane still in its airdrome.

A lever was now pulled and the undercarriage dropped to the ground while the *Atlantic,* freed from this weight, quickly rose high and left the land to its rear. Icebergs were sighted on the water and almost immediately the machine flew into the thick fog that for much of the year envelops the Newfoundland Banks. Up above this dense white cloudland the *Atlantic* rose and winged due east for four hours, when the aviators calculated they had come 400 miles from St. Johns and must be above the main track of steamships.

As darkness came on the weather altered. Rain began to beat on the plane and its occupants, large clouds sprang up before them, and the wind swept from the north. A wind such as this retarded speed, for the machine had to fly somewhat sideways, with its head to the wind, and could not keep a direct course. When they had flown about five hours Hawker noticed that the thermometer attached to the radiator stood unusually high, which appeared to indicate some difficulty with the circulation. If the water should boil and escape as steam the engine would become too hot to do its work.

Presently as they flew through the night sky they took observations by the stars and found that they had drifted southwards 150 miles from the course they had mapped, and therefore they had to head northeast to regain the proper line. In an effort to clear the obstruction from the radiator they tried diving towards the water and rising quickly again. So as not to overheat the engine they kept their pace down to "cruising" speed and their height of ascent to 12,000 feet.

Then there rose a great mass of storm-clouds, 15,000 feet high, in the course of the machine. They must climb above them, but as they climbed the radiator boiled and threw out steam that instantly turned to ice. They must try some other plan, so the plane was headed towards the water and ran into dense clouds. Hawker throttled down the engine until the airplane was only 1,000 feet above the sea; then, when he opened the throttle he found to his consternation that the engine would not respond.

The plane was almost in the water when the engine started up again and the situation was saved. Daylight glimmered on the ocean and the airmen took observations. Apparently they had flown about 950 miles at an average speed of about 85 miles an hour and had covered the greater part of the distance from Newfoundland to Ireland. But the radiator kept on heating and it was evident that the machine could not keep to its course through the sky but must land in the ocean. Hawker's object was to locate a ship; unless he could get near one there appeared little likelihood that the plane would be seen and picked up from the water.

No ships were visible in the dawn light, only a vast extent of ocean, kicked up into great waves by a boisterous wind. Hither and thither Hawker steered the plane, hunting for a vessel. The machine was tossed wildly by the gale and the waters leaped high below, as if they were attempting to drag the little airship down into their maw. Rain and fog added to the difficulty of seeing any distance, but at length Hawker spied a ship and started towards it. Catching up with it, he flew around it to attract the attention of the crew, then went on for a mile or so and brought the plane down to the ocean. The waves wrecked the top planes and broke over the machine, but it floated. Detaching their boat from the main body, Hawker and Mackenzie-Grieve waited for the ship—the steamer *Mary* of Copenhagen—to come up with them. Presently they were picked up by a boat from the steamer, but the *Atlantic* was left in the trough of the waves.

When they were rescued at 8 A. M. on May nineteenth the aviators had flown 1,050 miles from Newfoundland.

Six days later—on the morning of May twenty-fifth—the coastguards at the signal station on the Butt of Lewis, the most northern point of the Hebrides, sighted a small steamer, which hoisted flags giving her name: the *Mary* of Copenhagen. Other signal flags followed: "Communicate by wire"; and then "Saved hands—Sopwith airplane." Immediately the news of the rescue of the two aviators was telegraphed to London. As nothing had been heard of the *Atlantic* since she had left Newfoundland Hawker and Mackenzie-Grieve had been thought to have been lost in the ocean; the word that they were safe went flying joyously all over the world.

Later that day the two airmen were taken aboard a destroyer sent out from Scapa Flow to meet the steamer, and the following day they were landed at Thurso, the northern terminus of the Highland Railway. From there all the way to London the two were greeted by welcoming crowds. Arrived in the metropolis they were received at Buckingham Palace by King George, who bestowed on them the Royal Air Force Cross. Several days later a luncheon was given in their honor and a cheque for £5,000 was handed to the two aviators as a gift from the Daily Mail.

The machine in which they had almost crossed the Atlantic was picked up by an American ship and forwarded to England. At the time when the aviators had been forced to descend to the water half of the supply of gasoline was still in the tanks, and but for the trouble with the radiator the *Atlantic* would probably have been able to fly on to Ireland.

CHAPTER XII

THE AIRPLANE CROSSES THE ATLANTIC

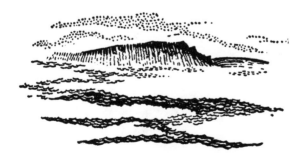

XII

THE AIRPLANE CROSSES THE ATLANTIC

WHILE Hawker and Mackenzie-Grieve were making their attempt in the *Atlantic* three flying-boats were voyaging across the ocean from west to east. These flying-boats were biplanes belonging to the United States Navy, and were numbered respectively NC1, NC3 and NC4. The hull of the boat body was divided into six compartments; the bow compartment was the navigator's cockpit, behind it was that in which two pilots sat, the next two compartments held the fuel and oil tanks, and in the stern was the wireless operator's station.

These flying-boats had started from Trepassey Bay, in Newfoundland, on May 16, 1919, two days before the *Atlantic* set out from St. Johns. Their route was to be from Newfoundland to the Azores, from the Azores to Lisbon, and from Lisbon to Plymouth, England, from which port the Pilgrims had sailed in the *Mayflower*. There was no intention of making a non-stop flight from America to Europe.

As guides and to render assistance if any were needed American destroyers were stationed at intervals of about 60 miles between Newfoundland and the Azores and British warships between the Azores and Lisbon. Wireless would enable the flying-boats to keep in touch with the ships and to receive reports on the weather conditions in various parts of the ocean.

They left Newfoundland at 10.05 P. M., and were soon flying over icebergs. The NC4, in charge of Lieutenant-Commander A. C. Read, presently outdistanced the other two, sighted Flores Island, the most westerly of the Azores, at 11.27 A. M. the next morning, and landed at Horta, in the island of Fayal, at 1.23 P. M. on May seventeenth. The flying-boat had covered 1,380 miles in 15 hours, 17 minutes, and had made an average speed of 81.7 knots.

The NC1 lost her bearings in a fog and came down in the water 200 miles west of the Azores, where her crew were picked up by a ship. The NC3 also had to alight in the ocean; no ship was near and the ocean was very rough; the flying-boat rode out a gale and then taxied over the water 205 miles to Ponta Delgada, where she arrived on May nineteenth. The machine was considerably damaged. As the NC1 had been left in the water after having been towed 80 miles, the NC4 was the only one of the three flying-boats to continue the voyage.

The NC4 spent three days at Horta, then flew to Ponta Delgada, where a week was given to preparations for the second leg of the trip. On May twenty-seventh the flying-boat rose from the Azores and flew safely to Lisbon, making the distance of 800 miles in 9 hours, 25 minutes. Lisbon, the first place in Europe to be reached by air from America, gave the NC4 a great welcome.

The flying-boat left Lisbon for Ferrol, in Spain, on May thirtieth, arrived at Ferrol, and next day headed across the Bay of Biscay for her goal in England. In the afternoon the English coast was sighted, the NC4 passed above the breakwater at the entrance to Plymouth Sound and successfully glided down into the harbor.

The Atlantic Ocean had now been crossed by a heavier-than-air machine, but the Daily Mail's prize had not yet been won by a non-stop flight. Hawker and Mackenzie-Grieve had not succeeded in flying across nor did the next contestants, the Englishmen Rayham and Morgan, who started from St. Johns about an hour after Hawker, but who were obliged to come down because of a broken axle. The third entrants for the prize were Captain John Alcock and Lieutenant Arthur Brown, who had both won honors as English aviators in the war. Their machine was a Vickers-Vimy standard bombing plane, changed to meet the requirements of a transatlantic flight, with tanks of a capacity to hold 865 gallons of gasoline and two 350 horsepower engines.

This airplane reached St. Johns, Newfoundland, in May, 1919. As the hangar in which it was to be housed had not arrived the parts were assembled in the open, where they were protected from the wind by temporary screens. On June ninth a trial flight was made and another on June twelfth; as both of these were satisfactory the tanks were filled for a transatlantic trip. The Vimy was ready on the evening of June thirteenth to make a start early the next morning, but a strong wind, blowing obliquely across the airdrome, delayed the flyers. Then the wind shifted to the west, and Captain Alcock, who was eager to set out before a rival Handley-Page machine should leave its airdrome at Harbor Grace, determined to get away. The chocks under the wheels were removed, the engines were opened out full, and at 4.28 P. M. (Greenwich time) on June 14, 1919, the Vimy began to move. The machine was so heavily loaded that it looked as if she would not be able to clear the obstructions at the end of the airdrome, but she rose above a fence and started to climb steadily. The crowd gave a great cheer as the plane soared higher and higher, over Cabot Tower on Signal Hill, above the waters of the harbor, and then eastward across the ocean.

Alcock and Brown fully appreciated the difficulties of attempting to fly 1,890 miles to the coast of Ireland. Success depended largely on the engines; if anything happened to one of these, repairs could be made in the air, but if both engines got out of order the Vimy would have to descend to the water. The plane was not a flying-boat nor was her course patrolled by friendly ships as had been the route of the NC4. The flyers had wished no such patrol, though it had been offered. They wanted to depend entirely on their own resources.

On their trial trips the aviators had ascertained that their plane had a maximum speed of 120 miles an hour. As they did not wish to crowd their engines too much they figured on flying at an average speed of 90 miles an hour, which would bring them to Ireland in about twenty hours, and allow a surplus of five hours' supply of gasoline.

Each of the flyers had brought along a black cat as mascot.

Brown, the navigator, had charted a direct course to Galway Bay, in Ireland. As the Vimy swept over the sea she gained in altitude until she was flying at a height of about 5,000 feet. A steady wind from the northwest sent the plane scudding along at a speed of over a hundred miles an hour. After a while Brown began to use his wireless outfit, sending out messages to St. Johns station; as he did this he noticed that the spark became smaller and less crackling; wondering if the apparatus were out of order, he set to work to examine it.

It seemed as if the trouble was in the generator, which was in the forward under-part of the fuselage and which received its energy from a wind-propeller that was situated outside. Neither the propeller nor the dynamo could be seen from the cockpit nor could they be reached when the plane was in the air. Brown, however, thought that if he could get out on the lower wing and crouch down he could see the wind-propeller. Therefore, although Alcock tried to persuade him not to take such a risk, the navigator crawled out from the cockpit and, holding by the guy-wires, let himself down upon the wing struts.

Here the wind nearly tore him loose; but he managed to crouch and look under the body of the plane. Only a part of the wind-propeller was to be seen, three of the four blades had been split, probably when the Vimy had risen in Newfoundland.

Without the propeller the wireless outfit was out of commission. The aviators could send no messages and receive none. Brown had intended to use a sextant to locate their position on the chart every Greenwich mean-time hour and send it broadcast, then to pick up weather reports relayed from Washington by ships which would enable them to avoid storms; without the wireless they could not have this invaluable assistance, they must rely for direction on sights taken at the moon and stars at night and the sun in the daytime and trust to avoid storms by the look of the sky and good fortune.

Soon they ran into a fog and could see nothing of sea or sky. Brown wanted to take a sight and asked Alcock to fly higher. Up the pilot steered and presently they were at a height of 12,000 feet. Here they could see the moon and stars. Brown took his observations and reported that they were too far north. The wind—on their starboard quarter—was drifting them from their course. "We'd better drop down

The Start of the First Non-Stop Flight Across
the Atlantic

The NC-4 Crossing the Atlantic by Way of the Azores

above the water," said the navigator, "and try to get the amount of drift from the waves."

The pilot sent the plane downward. The fog rolled about them. The Vimy went tearing along, blown now by a wind from the southwest. The aviators strained their eyes trying to see how near they were to the water; they had no wish to plunge headlong into the ocean.

Fortune came to their aid. By luck or by intuition Alcock eased off the elevator planes of the tail a moment before he saw the whitecaps under him and heard the swish of water. The Vimy straightened on an even keel just about twenty-five feet above the sea.

Brown looked through the lens in the bottom of the cockpit, but found that it magnified the waves too much. He looked over the side, was able to take a sight on a whitecap with his sextant, and so succeeded in determining how much the plane was drifting to the north of the proper course.

Then upward the pilot steered again, rose through the curtain of fog, and brought the plane into clear air at a height of 11,500 feet. Now they could gauge their direction better and flew on, sometimes through wisps of fog, but generally with the moon and stars to light the sky.

Such was the strength of the wind that the dial showed they were making 125 miles an hour, although Alcock was keeping the engines well throttled down, as he had been continually since the start of the voyage. The sky was clear for a while, then the moonlight and starlight dimmed and rain commenced to fall.

Rain would make it difficult or impossible to take observations; without observations the aviators would lose their way and be flying by guesswork. The rain grew denser and the atmosphere more cold. The water turned into sleet and the plane, from nose to tail and across the wings, was coated with ice.

The moon and stars vanished. The flyers frequently looked over the side of the cockpit to see how near they were to the ocean. They were steering now entirely by the compass and trusting to its accuracy. When they could they snatched hasty bites of sandwiches, hasty gulps of coffee. Through the pelting hail-storm they journeyed for four hours, then the clouds cleared sufficiently for Brown to take observations from the Pole Star and from the star Vega. They were north of their course; now they were able to correct their direction.

The sun rose. The machine had outridden the storm that had so encrusted it with ice that it crackled at every motion. The wind was still blowing strongly from the southwest and as the Vimy was flying at a rate of 128 miles an hour the aviators thought they must almost have crossed the Atlantic. Presently, however, they ran into fog. The fog-belt might not hang low, they thought, so Alcock steered down, and at a height of 300 feet above the water they came into clear air again.

Flying just below the fog, they sighted a ship at a distance but soon lost sight of the vessel. The fog came lower, and rather than fly too close to the water they soared again to get above the mist. At a height of 13,000 feet they were still in the fog and as the air was becoming very cold Alcock gave over trying to rise above the belt and set to work to steer by the compass on an even keel at 12,000 feet.

To fly on an even keel when one cannot see the horizon is a difficult task. Without a sense of the horizon the aviator becomes uncertain as to whether he is flying evenly or upward or downward. Alcock and Brown could only keep peering through the dense mist, looking up and down in the hope of sighting the water before they should be too close to it or of preventing the plane from taking a perpendicular position and toppling into a tail-spin.

To add to his sense of uncertainty Alcock thought that neither the speed indicator nor the altitude indicator was acting properly. He felt that the plane was going downward and immediately steered the machine up. They were actually rising, as it happened, when he did this, and consequently the Vimy in a moment was standing on end. Fortunately the engines were going at such a speed that the plane, instead of making a tail-spin, turned completely over and continued her course flying upside down.

The life-belts held the aviators in and the cats kept their position by clawing at the seats. For several minutes Alcock and Brown did not appreciate what had happened; when they did the pilot opened the throttle a little more and the plane made a half-loop and succeeded in reaching an even keel.

Next they suddenly emerged from the fog and almost dashed into the ocean. Alcock gave a quick thrust to the elevating-planes and they rose just above a big wave that pawed at them. Up they went and presently found that the fog was dissipating. Then they were able to take a sight by the sun. They were almost exactly on the course they had charted.

Delighted at this, they were even more delighted when soon afterwards they spied two small islands and located them on the map as Eastal and Turbot. Ten minutes and they saw the masts of the wireless station at Clifden, Ireland. Towards these they flew and around them they circled, looking for a suitable place to land. They saw what appeared to be a level green field and Alcock sent the plane swooping down to it. The field turned out to be a bog and as soon as the Vimy's wheels struck it they plowed into the mire. The plane stuck its nose in the mud and almost threw the aviators out of the cockpit. The wireless men from the Clifden station, running up, found Alcock and Brown somewhat dazed by the impact of the machine in the bog, but otherwise unhurt.

From the wireless station the aviators sent this message to the British Aero Club:

"Landed at Clifden at 8.40 A.M. Greenwich mean time, 15th of June, 1919, Vickers-Vimy Atlantic machine, leaving Newfoundland coast at 4.28 P.M. Greenwich mean time, 14th of June. Total time, 16 hours, 12 minutes.

Alcock and Brown."

The plane's engines, which had run faultlessly, had with the help of the wind driven the machine at an average rate of 118 miles an hour.

At Clifden and all along the route to London crowds poured congratulations on the two aviators who had made the first non-stop flight across the Atlantic Ocean. Praise for their great achievement came from many quarters. A luncheon was given in their honor in London and on this gala occasion Winston Churchill, the English Secretary of State for War, spoke for the Government.

"It is more than 400 years," he said, "since Columbus discovered America, it is only ten since Blériot flew the English Channel. . . . Think of the broad Atlantic, that terrible waste of desolate waters, tossing in tumult in repeated and almost ceaseless storms, and shrouded with an unbroken canopy of mist. Across this waste, and through this obscurity, two human beings, hurtling through the air, piercing the cloud and darkness, finding their unerring path in spite of every difficulty to their exact objective across those hundreds of miles, arriving almost on schedule time, and at every moment in this voyage liable to destruction from a drop of water in the carburetor, or a spot of oil on their plugs, or a tiny grain of dirt in their feed pipe, or from any of the other hundred and one indirect causes which in the present state of aeronautics might drag an airplane to its fate.

"When one considers all these factors I really do not know what we should admire the most in our guests—their audacity, their determination, their skill, their science, their Vimy-Vickers airplane, their Rolls-Royce engines, or their good fortune. All these were necessary, and all of them contributed to their achievement, and to the event which brought us all together here this afternoon, to cheer the victors of the first non-stop Atlantic flight."

King George awarded the Knight-Commandership of the Order of the British Empire to Captain Alcock and Lieutenant Brown.

The Vimy plane was dug out of the Irish bog and sent to London where, as an object of historic interest, it was given to the nation and placed in the Science Museum at South Kensington.

CHAPTER XIII

FROM LONDON TO AUSTRALIA

XIII

FROM LONDON TO AUSTRALIA

THE heroes of the Arabian Nights were accustomed to voyage through the air on magic carpets that wafted them over stupendous mountains, wide seas, and cities splendid with palaces and gardens. Those were wonderful adventures in the field of fancy; yet quite as marvellous was the actual journey by modern aviators from the English capital on the River Thames to the continent of Australia on the opposite side of the globe.

The Australian Commonwealth Government in 1919 offered a prize of £10,000 for the first flight by Australians from England to the Dominion in an airplane built of parts made entirely in the British Empire. It was further stipulated that the journey must be completed in 720 hours after the start, and must be made before the end of the year. The prize was a large one, but there were many hazards in a voyage through the air of 10,000 miles. Aviators had already flown from London as far as Calcutta and on this part of the route there were airdromes in France and Italy, and at Cairo, Damascus, Basra, Karachi, Delhi and Allahabad. East of Calcutta landing places were few and widely separated, there was no good airdrome except at Batavia, in Java, and the flight would be pioneer work.

Shortly after the war Brigadier-General A. E. Borton of the British Army had flown from Cairo to India and from there had visited by ship Burma, the Federated Malay States, Siam, Borneo and the Dutch East Indies, his object being to plan an air-route to Australia and arrange for landing places, fuel and other supplies, so that when he returned to India he might fly thence to Australia. It so happened, however, that during his absence his plane had been commandeered for use against the Afghans and been destroyed by a storm; therefore he had to abandon his projected trip.

On his journey in the Far East General Borton was accompanied by a young Australian aviator, Captain Ross Smith, and by two Australian air-mechanics, Sergeant J. M. Bennett and Sergeant W. H. Shiers. Captain Smith heard of the prize offered by the Australian Government and was eager to try to win it. He had a brother, Lieutenant Keith M. Smith, who was in England, and this brother would complete the crew of four that would be required for such a long and adventurous air voyage.

General Borton was recalled to London to make a report on the air-route he had surveyed in the Far East, and it was through his influence that Captain Ross Smith was able to secure from the manufacturers a Vickers-Vimy two-engined plane of the same type as that in which Alcock and Brown had flown across the Atlantic Ocean in the early summer of that year. A great deal of work had to be done in a short time, as the voyage from England to Australia must be accomplished before the end of 1919, maps and information of all sorts about the country to be traversed had to be obtained, supplies of gasoline and landing places arranged for. The aid of the Governor-General of the Dutch East Indies was secured, and this proved of the greatest value, since the provision of an airdrome at Bima, in the island of Sumbawa, and of another at Atamboea, in Timor, made it unnecessary to carry in any one stage of the journey more gasoline than would be used in a 1,000-mile flight, even under adverse conditions.

The machine that was to be used by Captain Ross Smith—officially known as the G-EAOU—was a biplane, with twin engines of 350 horsepower. In addition to the crew of four men the plane was to carry over 500 gallons of gasoline, 40 gallons of oil, water, tools, repair kit, and emergency rations of food sufficient to last for a week in case a landing had to be made where food would be unobtainable.

On November 11, 1919, the plane was flown from the works at Weybridge to the Hounslow airdrome, which was the official starting-place. The following day five parts of the machine were officially marked and sealed, as it was a stipulation of the competition that only one airplane was to be used by any one crew, and that three of the five marked parts must be intact at the end of the voyage.

The machine rose at 8 A. M. and was off from England to Australia. Weather conditions were not of the best, thick mists covered the English fields, and the aviators had no view of the country until they were over Folkestone when the sun broke through the fog and showed the white caps of the Channel in a brisk wind. In France the biplane ran into a storm of sleet and snow, that was numbingly cold. The elevator was put up, the plane rose in a spiral, and at a height of 9,000 feet came into brilliant sunshine. Up above the clouds the route could not be followed by landmarks and the compass was the sole guide to steer the course to Lyons, which was to be the first landing place.

In descending the plane encountered the storm, a gale so cold that even the sandwiches were frozen. Flying was no easy matter in such an icy atmosphere, but fortunately an opening showed in the clouds and spiralling down this the Vimy came into clear air. The aviators made out the town of Roanne from its location on the map, and went on easily to Lyons, a distance of 40 miles, where they made a safe landing.

The weather over France was more favorable the next day and the course was laid for Marseilles and the Riviera. The Maritime Alps came into view, a magnificent line of cloud-capped, rocky peaks. Then the wonderful blue of the Mediterranean was beneath the plane and the route was shifted to the east over Cannes, Monte Carlo and San Remo, and now, above Italy, across the Gulf of Genoa to Spezia. The schedule called for Rome as the next landing place, but a strong headwind cut down their speed; Rome could not be reached before dark of the short November day, and so the aviators descended for their second landing at the Pisa airdrome.

The ground here was soaking wet, and the next day was so damp that the plane could not take the air, sticking in the mud when the engines were started. The following morning, November fifteenth, was equally wet and at the first attempt of a take-off the Vimy became so embedded that the wheels had to be dug out and the plane hauled from the mud. On the next try the plane rolled slowly forward and would not rise until one of the mechanics climbed on to the tail and kept her down while she gained sufficient speed to lift from the ground. The mechanic was then pulled on board, and the Vimy sailed away and in spite of boisterous headwinds succeeded in arriving that evening at the city on the Tiber.

From Rome the plane flew next morning south over Naples, with cloud-wreathed Vesuvius on the one hand, and then east over the Apennines, a rough and rugged country, where the air was "bumpy," and flying was "bumpy" too. Across the mountains the Vimy made a halt at the seaport of Taranto, where Captain Ross Smith and his party were warmly welcomed by officers of the Royal Air Force, stationed at one of the principal airdromes on the London-Cairo route. The mechanics busied themselves with tuning up the plane for the next hop, a stretch of 520 miles to Suda Bay on the north side of Crete, of which a large distance would be over the Mediterranean.

The journey on the following day, November seventeenth, should have furnished marvellous views to the voyagers through the air as they crossed the sea to Corfu and flew along the romantic coast of Greece; rain fell in torrents, however, and made steering so difficult that the pilot almost sent the plane crashing into a cliff that suddenly loomed from the mist. Luckily he was able to bring the Vimy round at a right-angle, otherwise the attempt to fly to Australia would have ended on the rocky Grecian shore.

The rain continued until the plane headed out from the southern point of Greece over open water towards the island of Crete. Here was the world of legends; this was the air through which, according to the ancient fable, Dædalus and Icarus flew with wings fastened to their shoulders by wax. As the wings of the modern flying man, the wings of the Vimy biplane, soared across from Greece the rain clouds fell behind and the aviators had a wonderful view of Crete, the peaks of its great ridge of mountains lying purple and golden in the brilliant sunlight. Not attempting to imitate Icarus by flying too near the sun, they circled above the town of Canea and brought the plane down easily to the Suda airdrome.

Early the next day the party were off, for a drenching rain was falling, which threatened to make the airdrome a muddy, sticky mass from which it would be difficult to rise. Flight over the island of Crete presented a problem to the aviators; the mountain range extended from shore to shore and rose in places to above 8,000 feet. These heights were hidden in clouds, and in order to avoid striking them the plane must either be piloted very high or be navigated through some pass below the clouds. Captain Smith found a pass that served his purpose and the Vimy sailed away over the 250 miles of open water that separated Crete from the coast of Africa. The sea was traversed in about three hours and the plane went winging over bare, sandy land, eastward from the port of Sollum and along the coast in the direction of Cairo. The Pyramids came into sight, and after a run of 650 miles for the day the Vimy landed in the Heliopolis airdrome.

It had taken seven days to reach Africa from England, and the aviators had flown almost 2,500 miles of the total distance of 11,060 between London and Port Darwin in Australia. They had been able to keep up to their schedule, although the weather conditions had been trying. The next section of the journey, the 4,150 miles from Cairo to Calcutta, being mainly over plains and sea was not apt to offer many difficulties and moreover had already been navigated in air by three of Captain Smith's party.

When they landed at the airdrome they heard that M. Poulet, a French aviator who had left Paris with a companion in October in a Caudron biplane with the intention, if possible, of being the first to fly from Europe to Australia, had arrived in India. He was not in the competition for the prize of the Australian Government, but if he should succeed in getting to Port Darwin before Captain Smith's party reached there the latter would lose some of the glory of their pioneer trip. The Frenchman had a start of some thousands of miles on the Australians, but they determined to try to overtake him, and therefore, instead of resting up for a day at Cairo, they set off early next morning for Damascus.

Flying above the Ismailia Canal they had a magnificent view of the Nile Delta; they crossed the Suez Canal, winged above Kantara, and went on over the Sinai desert, where for miles and miles they saw only the sand, the railway tracks and the pipeline to Gaza. Here was a country it had taken the Children of Israel forty years to traverse, but the Vimy biplane did it in forty minutes. Gaza, Jerusalem, the Dead Sea, the Jordan Valley were safely crossed and from the Sea of Galilee the aviators saw the snow-clad, glistening peaks of Mount Hermon and the Anti-Libanus. There followed another stretch of sandy desert, and then there came into sight the green of verdure and amid it the walls of Damascus. Here they alighted at the airdrome in one of the world's most ancient and most famous cities.

Rain was falling next day, and, lest a muddy field should hinder the plane's start, they got away from

Damascus as early as they could. Bagdad was to be the next port of call, according to their schedule,— that city about which were woven so many of the tales in the Arabian Nights,—and the course lay over the ruins of the majestic city of Palmyra and along the Euphrates, the great waterway from Syria to the Persian Gulf. Headwinds prevented them from making speed, so about sunset they decided to alight at Ramadie, 40 miles from Bagdad, where an Indian cavalry regiment had its headquarters. At Ramadie a gale rose during the night, blowing from such a quarter that it threatened to lift the Vimy by the tail and turn it over, which might easily have ruined it. The aviators and the soldiers rushed out, seized the plane and pulled it around with its head to the wind. The ailerons on the wings broke their control wires and would have been badly injured by the buffeting of the gale had not the rescuers quickly tied them in place. Next morning, however, the wind, which had so nearly wrecked their plans, proved a boon to Captain Smith's party, for it blew in the direction they were travelling and sent them at a greater speed than they had yet made. Over Bagdad they flew—not stopping there, as they had been able to obtain fresh supplies of gasoline at Ramadie— and over Ctesiphon and Kut el Amara. They were flying southeast over Mesopotamia, and within three hours arrived at Basra, at the head of the Persian Gulf, where they landed at the airdrome and where they spent the next day overhauling the engines.

From Basra the Vimy rose at dawn on November twenty-third, her next stop planned to be made at Bandar Abbas, 630 miles to the south, at the entrance to the Persian Gulf. Conditions were perfect, there was a following wind and the brilliant sunshine gave a splendid view of the wide waters of the Gulf and of the shores of Persia on the eastern side. Those shores were filled with gullys and dry watercourses and there was no place where an airplane could safely land, but the Vimy flew smoothly onward, engines working to perfection, and descended easily at Bandar Abbas, where a large crowd of natives joyfully welcomed the travellers from afar.

The next flight, from Bandar Abbas to Karachi, in India, was 730 miles, the longest single jump of the whole journey. The route lay over the coast of the Arabian Sea and above the bare, wild country of southern Persia and Baluchistan. Following the shore until they were within one hundred miles of the goal, the aviators then headed straight across the water and reached the airdrome at Karachi $8\frac{1}{2}$ hours after the start of the day's flight. Here they learned that their rival, the Frenchman Poulet, was at Delhi, only one day's journey ahead of them.

The Vimy was off for Delhi, more than 700 miles to the east, early next morning. For three hours they flew over the desert of Sind, then came to a vast country of green, irrigated land. The air was bumpy here and the plane wallowed like a ship in the trough of the waves. They made Delhi by nightfall and now had completed one-half of the voyage.

Poulet was still a day's stage ahead of them, having arrived at Allahabad. In the last three days, however, Captain Smith's party had covered almost 2,100 miles and were worn with the strain, therefore they rested for a day, and on the next flew across the Central Plains. When they reached Allahabad they heard that their rival had gone on to Calcutta.

In Calcutta the next day they were given a great reception. By arriving in the capital of Bengal they had flown 6,500 miles from England and there were 4,500 miles to be flown to Australia. Poulet was still in the lead, he had set out that morning for Akyab, in Burma.

When the Vimy rose next day from the race course at Calcutta a small accident almost proved her undoing. She had to surmount some tall trees and while she was ascending a couple of hawks flew into the propellers. Almost any object, no matter how small, lodging in a propeller that is rotating at some hundreds of revolutions a minute may make the propeller fly into pieces; if the Vimy's propeller broke, the plane would crash into the trees. In this instance no damage was done, although the pilot, in trying to steer away from other hawks, almost ran the plane into a tree. Thereafter all went well, the Vimy crossed the forests, streams and swamps of the delta of the Ganges—a tract of a couple of hundred miles where there was no place to land—and flew to the coast of Burma at Chittagong. There she turned south to Akyab. As they neared the airdrome at that place the Australians saw a small plane already there; it was the Caudron of Poulet. Their French rival was the first to greet them when they landed. From Akyab on it would be a neck-and-neck race between the two planes to Australia.

The Frenchman set out first for Rangoon on November thirtieth and had an hour's start on the Australians. The Vimy kept to the coast for about one hundred miles and then, shifting to the east, crossed a mountain range and followed the Irrawady River south towards Prome. Picking up the railway line there, the plane flew above it to the capital of Burma, where people from miles around Rangoon had collected to see this strange machine and to welcome the men who voyaged in it. An hour after the Vimy's arrival Poulet descended at Rangoon in his machine and was enthusiastically greeted by the Burmese, who were greatly interested in the race between the two planes.

There was plenty of excitement next morning, for when the Vimy made her take-off from the race course the undercarriage of the plane swept across the tops of the trees. The Australians had intended to fly with their French rival to the next landing place at Bangkok, the capital of Siam, but the engine of Poulet's machine was out of order and the Frenchman had to wait to repair it.

Captain Smith set his course over the Gulf of

Martaban to Moulmein and then southeasterly across the mountains that divide Burma from Siam. Some of this range rise from 6,000 to 7,000 feet above sea level, and as the tops were covered by clouds the Vimy had to climb high to avoid striking them. When she was at a height of 11,000 feet the Vimy was still in the clouds and could only gauge her course by the compass. Navigation became difficult. Once the plane almost got out of control and headed downward towards the mountains. She was righted, however, and presently, when the pilot thought that the highest peaks might have been surmounted, he allowed the machine to glide down to an elevation of some 7,000 feet. The crew kept a sharp lookout. They caught sight of something dark breaking through the clouds. Instantly the Vimy "zoomed" to avoid striking a mountain. Then it was seen that the dark object was a glimpse of country showing through a hole in the clouds; the range was probably passed, and the machine was allowed to glide lower until at a height of 4,000 feet she emerged into clear air and saw below her a forest that stretched to the horizon. This forest country was a wild and unexplored tract, but after flying over it for an hour the Vimy came to cultivated land along the Mekong River. With great relief—for the flight from Burma to Siam over cloud-hidden mountains was one of the most difficult and hazardous parts of the journey— the aviators alighted at the Muang airdrome, some miles north of Bangkok.

Bangkok to Singapore was to be the next hop, according to the schedule, but Captain Smith learned that there was an airdrome at Singora, on the Malay Peninsula, situated about midway between the two cities, which were separated a distance of between 900 and 1,000 miles. He decided to stop here and divide the journey. Heavy, tropical rain fell as they flew from Bangkok, a deluge that drenched and almost blinded the aviators, and once the Vimy was nearly wrecked—there was a narrow escape from collision with a rocky headland that stuck out from the coast. When they reached the airdrome at Singora the crew saw that it was half under water and moreover was filled with the stumps of trees. It was the only landing place, however, so down the Vimy glided. By great good fortune she missed the stumps and the only damage sustained was the loss of the tail skid, which the mechanics were able to replace.

That night a gale blew and rain fell in torrents, so the aviators had to stay by the machine to prevent her being wrecked by drifting in the water. Next morning an army of 200 convicts cleared the airdrome of the tree-stumps and a supply of gasoline was brought from Penang. December fourth the aviators succeeded in getting away from water-logged Singora, flew above the rubber plantations of British Malaya, and landed at Singapore. The rain had made the race-course here almost a swamp, and there was little room to alight or take-off, on account of the close-ranged houses and trees. The plane got away, however, and flew above the coast to Sumatra, over country so thickly wooded that there was no place for landing for 200 miles. Then she laid her course across the open sea, and finished the nine hours' flight from Singapore by landing in the airdrome at Kalidjati, near Batavia, the capital of Java.

The next landing place was at Surabaya, in eastern Java. The airdrome here had been built on reclaimed land and there was a thin, hard coating on the top of very soft mud. When she alighted the Vimy broke through the coating and became engulfed in mire; by dint of a great deal of digging and pulling the machine was freed, but again squashed into the swamp. Mats of bamboo were placed under the wheels and there was more digging and pulling. The plane was hauled out a second time, but two tires were punctured and the jacks that were put under the carriage to raise it for repairing the tires kept sinking into the mud. The aviators were in a quandary: they had flown all but 1,200 miles of the distance to Australia, and here they were stuck at Surabaya. Then Captain Smith had a happy idea: if they could get enough bamboo mats they might build a roadway over which the Vimy's wheels would run without sticking in the mire. With the help of a local official the aviators procured a great supply of mats—many of which were the walls of Surabaya houses—and constructed a road 300 yards in length.

The engines were started in the morning and the plane was steered over the road, but as she went forward the draught made by the propellers lifted the mats in the rear and these fouled the machine's tail so that she ran off the track and plunged into the mud.

After a great deal more digging and hauling the Vimy was brought again to the starting place. The mats were now tied together and fastened tightly by pegs to the ground. Again the motors whirred, the machine ran over the pathway, and this time she rose successfully and flew off towards Bima, in the island of Sambawa.

Atamboea, in the island of Timor, was reached on December ninth, and only 450 miles of open sea remained to be crossed to reach the Australian coast. For this last lap of the journey the British warship *Sydney* had been detailed to patrol the water under the airplane. On December tenth the Vimy rose, brushed against the tops of trees, and then was off and away. As she flew across the sea the aviators caught sight of the *Sydney* and swooped down close enough to hear the cheers of the sailors. Then the plane left the warship and the Australian fliers looked southward for the first glimpse of their homeland. Just before 2 P. M. they sighted a distant haze; it was Bathurst Island lighthouse. On sped the Vimy, and at 3 P. M. the plane landed in Australia after a voyage of 27 days, 20 hours.

The prize had been won. The stipulation of the award was that the journey should be completed in 720 hours after the start; it had actually been made with 52 hours to spare. As for the gallant French rival, M. Poulet, he had been outdistanced, and Captain Smith's party had the honor of being the first to fly from Europe to Australia.

Port Darwin gave the aviators a royal welcome. The cities of Sydney, Melbourne and Adelaide wanted a sight of the famous plane and its indomitable crew, so the Vimy set out again, to fly the continent from north to south. Repairs had to be made during the journey and it was more than three months after they had started before they had flown the 3,500 miles from Port Darwin to Adelaide, which was the Smiths' native city. At Melbourne the Prime Minister presented the aviators with the prize of £10,000 and the Vimy was turned over to the Commonwealth Government. In recognition of their great achievement Captain Ross Smith and his brother, Lieutenant Keith M. Smith, were knighted by King George V.

The journeys through the air of the heroes of the Arabian Nights had been surpassed by the voyage of the Vimy's crew of four modern aviators from England to Australia.

CHAPTER XIV

FROM CAIRO TO THE CAPE

XIV

FROM CAIRO TO THE CAPE

SOON after the signing of the Armistice at the end of the war in November, 1918, three parties of surveyors set out to explore the central part of Africa, with the object of locating places that would be suitable for airdromes. The sites that were selected were then to be cleared and depots of gasoline and other supplies were to be established for the use of airplanes, as it was intended to discover whether the Dark Continent could be traversed from north to south by aircraft in ordinary conditions.

Many difficulties beset this work; there was the tropical heat, the poisonous insects and wild animals, the travel through jungles and swamps, and the need of guarding against the possible enmity of native tribes, whose assistance must be secured for the labor of clearing the airdrome sites. The surveyors were officers detailed by the British Air Ministry, and they did their work with such skill and vigor that within a year they had completed their mission and as a result there was a chain of twenty-three airdromes and nineteen emergency landing grounds between Cairo and Cape Town.

The most northerly of these stations was at Heliopolis, near Cairo, and south of that there were stations at Assiut and Assouan on the Nile. From Wady Halfa to Atbara and thence to Khartoum the aerial chain ran. Continuing through the Sudan and central Africa there were many stations, one at Abercorn on Lake Tanganyika, and another at Jinja on the Victoria Nyanza. On the south the links connected Bulawayo, Pretoria, Johannesburg, Bloemfontein, Victoria West and Cape Town at the Cape of Good Hope.

The route measured 5,206 miles from Heliopolis to Cape Town and the average distance between stations—airdromes and emergency landing grounds—was 124 miles.

An expedition to attempt a flight from Cairo to the Cape was then organized under the sponsorship of England's great newspaper, the Times. The Air Ministry assisted, and so did the airplane builders, Messrs. Vickers, Ltd., who furnished a twin-engined Vickers-Vimy machine of the type that had been used in the voyage across the Atlantic by Alcock and Brown and in the long-distance journey from London to Australia of Captain Ross Smith and his party.

The leader of this new flight was Dr. P. Chalmers-Mitchell, an eminent scientist and secretary of the Zoölogical Society. The pilots were Captain S. Cockerell and Captain F. C. Broome; and the crew was completed by Sergeant-Major James Wyatt as mechanic and Mr. C. Corby as rigger.

The expedition aroused great interest. Would the

aviators be able to follow the route of the airdromes?
A forced landing might easily jeopardize the machine, as well as imperil the party from strange
tribes and wild beasts. Central Africa, moreover, was
a country of tropical storms, and in one of these
gales the airplane might be blown into a swamp or
jungle. It was a decidedly sporting proposition that
the aviators were engaged on.

The plane set out from Brooklands, in England,
on January 24, 1920, and after a somewhat stormy
trip reached Heliopolis, the airdrome for Cairo, on
February first. On February sixth it rose before a
cheering crowd, and circling to gain height, pointed
its nose southward on the first lap of its long journey
over river and desert, forest and jungle, to the Cape.

The weather was fine and the Vimy flew above
the Nile until it reached Luxor, where it had to descend as one of the engines had become overheated.
A cylinder had sprung a leak, which had let out the
water intended to cool the engine. The leak was soon
repaired, the machine was started again, and the
journey continued that day to Assouan. As they flew
above the Nile country the aviators could see to the
west the vast extent of the Libyan desert, a track-
less, waterless, and uninhabited plain, to the east
of the river were stretches of rocks and sand, and at
Assouan the wonderful dam that stores up the water
of the Nile for use in fertilizing the country in the
dry seasons.

The engines needed adjusting and so a day was

spent in this work at Assouan. February eighth the flight was resumed towards Khartoum. Sometimes the aviators followed the Nile, sometimes were able to take short cuts where the river turned. Again a leak let out water and a landing was made at one of the emergency grounds. Repaired, the machine soared aloft and winged over deserts and the craters of extinct volcanoes. Here the heat was very great and one of the engines became too hot for use. The pilot changed his course towards the Nile and managed to bring the plane down a few miles from the river on fairly level ground. The place was deserted and it took considerable time to find a native, who was despatched to fetch water on a camel. With the engine in proper working order and the water replenished, the plane went on and arrived that evening at Khartoum, after a flight of 618 miles for the day.

The next day was given over to work on the engines and to cleaning out a great accumulation of dust in the body of the machine. The following morning the party set out from Khartoum, their intention being to fly that day as far as Mongalla, which is on the upper reaches of the White Nile. To get to that place they would have to cross great stretches of swamps, those morasses of fetid vegetation into which the Nile broadens. An unhealthy country this and mostly uninhabited. The wind that morning helped them to fly 208 miles in two hours to Jebelein, on the Nile, and there they alighted to fill the tanks with gasoline and remedy a small leak. They had not flown far from Jebelein when there was some trouble with the magneto and they were forced to land in a dry swamp. Repair work took up the afternoon; that night they had to camp where they were. The air here was very cold and leopards prowled about their fire and the roars of other wild animals could be heard from the jungle. When they started in the morning an engine again sprang a leak and the pilots turned back to make repairs at Jebelein; the great swampy area was no region to attempt with an engine out of condition.

Three days were spent at Jebelein. The engines had been so continually leaking that the aviators considered giving up the attempt to fly south. An apparatus was devised, however, to pump water into the radiators from an extra tank, which might offset the leakage, and the party decided to push on and trust to this device to see them through.

The plane then left Jebelein on February fourteenth and made for Mongalla, which was 538 miles to the south and on the other side of the great swampy tract. The next landing place on the surveyors' route was at Eliri, which lay to the southwest, but instead of heading for this the pilot took the direct course to Mongalla. To do this necessitated the crossing a greater extent of the morasses. As they flew along above the swamp clouds of smoke arose from bush fires and made it difficult to see the ground and get proper bearings. The Nile had disappeared.

Presently the heat became so great that the engines, in spite of the new reserve supply, ran out of water; the plane must land somewhere. Hunting about, the pilot spied a piece of burnt ground in the jungle and on this he was able to land. There was no water in the vicinity, however. The party started to search and Corby, who had been left to guard the machine, was presently surrounded by natives, uncouth-looking tribesmen armed with bows and arrows. He offered them cigarettes and they showed no hostility, on the contrary, became quite friendly.

To find water was all important, so the airplane was set going again, and brought down on another burnt patch that was near a creek. The water here was not suitable, and another flight was made to a dry swamp near the Nile. Crocodiles, centipedes and mosquitoes infested this place. Natives arrived to inspect the strangers and the aviators induced one of them to go on foot to Mongalla to bring a supply of gasoline. In that dry swamp they camped for the night on board the plane, so as to be out of reach of crocodiles; and when in the morning the gasoline-bearer had not arrived Dr. Chalmers-Mitchell and Captain Broome started through swamp and jungle with a native to guide them to Mongalla. They arrived there after a tramp of six hours through equatorial heat, and found that Captain Worsley at Mangalla had received the note they had sent by the native and had set off in a canoe with fifty gallons of gasoline to rescue the aviators. With this supply

Captain Cockerell was able to get the plane up into the air from the swamp and in ten minutes flew over the route to Mongalla which it had taken his companions six hours to cover on foot.

The expedition stayed five days at Mongalla, for much work had to be done on the engines of the machine and this was rendered difficult by the great heat of equatorial Africa. The heat practically made the gasoline boil in the tanks, and on the first attempt to start for the station at Kisumu on February twentieth the shutters of the radiator would not work as the high temperature had made the wires that opened them slack. To remedy this the shutters were locked open. The plane then started away; presently the heat caused another misadventure, a burned-out inlet valve. This necessitated landing on the field at Nimule. In landing a tire was punctured, the flattened tire made the plane swing round and this broke the spring on the tail skid. The injuries were repaired and the party camped at Nimule, with a blazing fire to keep off the lions that roared in the tall grass.

The heat so rarefied the air that the plane could not gain height on the attempt to leave Nimule the next afternoon. The following day, however, the party were able to get away at dawn. They made a successful flight, crossed the Victoria Nile at Murchison Falls, and reached Jinja, where there was an airdrome on the north shore of the Victoria Nyanza. Next morning they started for Kisumu, but the magnetos gave trouble and they had to put back to the airdrome to straighten them out. They had had so many mishaps with various parts of the machinery that they might well have been discouraged, but they were cheered by the news that new engines were to be had at Kisumu.

They succeeded in reaching that station, which is the terminus of the Uganda Railway on the Victoria Nyanza, on February twenty-fourth. Eagerly they inquired for the new engines. As it turned out the engines, instead of being new, had been salvaged from a ship that had been sunk in salt water for three months and were in consequence quite unusable. The old engines therefore were overhauled and the plane made as light as possible for the journey over high altitudes south of the Victoria Nyanza.

On February twenty-sixth the aviators battled against a head wind to Mwanza, at the southern end of the lake. There they refilled the gasoline tanks and flew on to Tabora, in the Tanganyika Territory, which they reached that night. The next day the airplane ascended, but as it rose one of the engines got into trouble and the pilot had to descend into the bush where there were great anthills. One of the wheels was torn off and the machine was so much damaged that it was unfit for further service. The great adventure of a flight from Cairo to the Cape came to an end at Tabora, largely because of the effect of the great heat on the engines and magnetos. The party had covered 2,700 miles in an actual flying

Night and Day through all weathers the Mail Plane must fly

time of 36½ hours, an average speed of 75 miles an hour.

Africa was yet to be conquered in a north-to-south flight. The second attempt to win that triumph was made by two South African aviators, Lieutenant-Colonel Pierre van Ryneveld and Flight Lieutenant Brand, who left Brooklands in England on February fourth, flying a Vickers-Vimy christened the *Silver Queen*. They met with a terrific gale above the Mediterranean, but reached Cairo safely after battling with the wind for eleven hours. On February tenth they started out fom Cairo, their plan being to reach Khartoum, a distance of 1,044 miles, in a single flight. They had flown more than half of this journey when they encountered the same difficulties that had beset the first party; water leaked from a radiator and they had to make a forced descent in darkness on ground covered with rocks. The airplane was wrecked, but the aviators and the engines were undamaged. The landing was made at Korosko, on the Nile, and the two airmen returned to Cairo with the engines, and there installed them in a new plane, the *Silver Queen II*.

From the Heliopolis airdrome they set out in this new machine on February twenty-second. This time they succeeded in reaching Khartoum by nightfall. There they had to stop to repair the leaks, which appeared to be a regular incident of African air-travel. Proceeding south, they arrived at Mwanza on the twenty-sixth, and three days later flew over Tabora, where the Chalmers-Mitchell machine had been wrecked on February twenty-seventh and where those stranded pioneer aviators were still waiting for a train on the railroad to take them to the coast.

The *Silver Queen II* coursed through the air without mishap as far as Bulawayo, in Rhodesia. The machine had flown 3,880 miles in thirteen days. On rising from the Bulawayo airdrome, however, the *Silver Queen II* crashed to the ground and so ended her flight. The two South African pilots waited until a new plane, a de Haviland 9, was sent up from Cape Town, and in this they set out on March twentieth and completed their journey to the Cape. The flight took them just four weeks, including the stop of eleven days at Bulawayo.

In 1925 Alan J. Cobham was commissioned by Imperial Airways, Ltd., to survey an air route from Cairo to the Cape. This aviator had already many successful long distance flights to his credit, the most famous of which was a journey from London to Rangoon and return, a distance of 17,000 miles, which he had accomplished in an actual flying time of 220 hours.

For his African trip Cobham selected a de Haviland machine of the same type he had used in his Rangoon journey. In this he installed a 385 horsepower "Jaguar" engine, since the plane would have to make take-offs in rarefied air from airdromes that were situated many thousands of feet above sea level. This engine was of the radial air-cooled type, and the use of it would determine whether it was more efficient in tropical conditions than the water-cooled engines of the planes that had attempted to cross Africa in earlier flights.

Cobham, with a mechanic and a photographer with a motion-picture apparatus, left Stag Lane airdrome, Edgeware, England, in his plane on November 16, 1925. The expedition, whose object was to report on air conditions, topography and other scientific matters, as well as to make photographs, flew leisurely from place to place, and ultimately reached Cape Town on February 17, 1926. They had journeyed 8,500 miles and had actually been in the air 94 hours. By this trip Cobham gained the triumph of being the first to fly from London to Cape Town in the same machine with the same engine.

The party made a short stop at Cape Town and then started on a homeward flight, with the ambition to establish a record for a trip against time. Leaving Cape Town early on February twenty-sixth, they reached Kimberley that day. The next day they arrived at Bulawayo, after having dodged several heavy rainstorms and seen a procession of twenty lions on the march. Rain followed the aviators until they came to the Sudan country. Then instead of rain there was heat, 90° F. in the shade at a height of 7,000 feet and 160° in the sun near the ground. The flyers sheltered themselves under screens and flew on to Khartoum.

Beyond Khartoum they met a sandstorm and even

at an altitude of 12,000 feet could only see a few yards. Cobham made a landing and discovered a dry watercourse, which they followed and which eventually led them to the Nile. Where the river makes a great bend between Abu Hamed and Wady Halfa they flew low and steered by the railroad tracks and telegraph poles for over 200 miles. Then again the Nile guided them; in one day they made 480 miles in 4¾ hours; and on March seventh landed at Heliopolis. This flight of 5,500 miles—the first to be made from south to north across the continent—had been completed in 9½ days.

From Cairo Cobham flew on to London. His journey to that city from Cape Town was made in less than fifteen days. The Cape of Good Hope had been linked to Cairo and to England by the air route and the "Jaguar" engine had proved itself marvellously reliable in tropical heat and in blistering sandstorms.

CHAPTER XV

ACROSS NORTH AMERICA

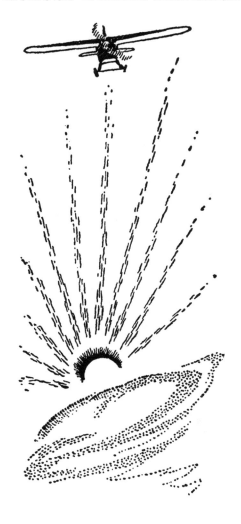

XV

ACROSS NORTH AMERICA

TO cross the continent of North America in a non-stop flight was the ambition of Lieutenants Oakley G. Kelly and John A. Macready, of the United States Army Air Service. Both men were experienced aviators and Macready held the world's altitude record of 34,509 feet. The original idea was Kelly's and when he suggested it to Macready the latter enthusiastically agreed to make the trip with him. For the journey they selected a Transport T2, a monoplane of the Fokker type, driven by a single Liberty engine of 420 horsepower. This plane would carry 557 gallons of gasoline in tanks inside the wings and another 180 gallons in a large tank in the fuselage, a quantity estimated to be sufficient for the transcontinental flight if the winds did not hold them back.

Both the aviators favored flying from east to west, but the Chief of the Weather Bureau at Washington recommended flying from the Pacific coast to the Atlantic, as the prevailing winds blow in that direction. There was one important objection to this; the aviators would meet the highest mountains on their route early in the flight, when the load of gasoline would not be sufficiently reduced to make high flying possible, and they would have to travel through passes which might be difficult to negotiate safely if the weather were cloudy. However, on account of the prevailing winds they decided to fly eastward.

With weather conditions reported as favorable the aviators started from Rockwell Field, San Diego, early on the morning of October 5, 1922, intending to fly to Long Island, New York, 2,700 miles across the continent. The plane was so heavily loaded that it ran almost a mile along the ground before it began to rise. Circling twice to gain altitude, Lieutenant Kelly, who was acting as pilot, laid a course due north for Temecula Pass, 50 miles distant. The machine cleared the pass, although the fog was thick, and flew on northeastward until it neared San Jacinto, where the fog enveloped it completely and the route could not be located. To try to fly on through the winding mountain passes in such a heavily loaded plane with fog so dense was too hazardous to attempt, so the aviators turned back towards San Diego, planning to change their cross-country flight to an endurance test which would give them information in regard to the consumption of gasoline, oil and water, and perhaps allow them to break the world's endurance record for airplanes.

When they were over Rockwell Field they dropped a message telling their plans, and then continued to circle above San Diego. Each of the two acted as pilot for six hours at a time, while the other rested. All that day and that night—there was a full moon

—and the next day they flew, then as their supply of gasoline was running low they descended while the ground was still visible and were surrounded by an applauding crowd that told them they had been flying for 35 hours 18 minutes and had broken the world's record by more than eight hours. This was a satisfaction, for they had demonstrated their ability to stay in the air a longer period than it was expected would be required for the transcontinental flight.

The aviators wanted to start again, but the weather was not favorable that October, and it was not until November third that the Weather Bureau reported that conditions were propitious. At dawn next morning the airmen ascended, flew several miles out to sea to gain height, and then set out for the mountains. They easily negotiated the Temecula Pass this time and crossed the mountain ranges as far as Banning in California. Flying over the Salton Sea they winged for 400 miles above the barren country through which the Colorado River has cut deep canyons. As they neared Tucson the ground rose to the spurs of the Rocky Mountains and the T2 was barely able to rise above the summits; the atmosphere was also very rough and bumpy, with numerous air currents that tossed the plane up and down hundreds of feet and made it very difficult for the pilot to guide his craft.

On they went over the alkali dry lakes and the great salt marshes of New Mexico, over the Malapais, or volcanic lava beds, over the mud huts of villages of Indians, who viewed with amazement this strange new bird. Near Tecelote a down current of air drove them towards the earth, which they missed by a small margin. To surmount a summit they made a detour and tried the height at a greater altitude; the second attempt failed, but on the third the T2 cleared the top with about 30 feet to spare. For some time they lost their bearings, but presently saw the lights of the small town of Tucumcari and were able to locate their position again on the map.

The vast prairies of Oklahoma and Kansas unrolled before them and the peril of the mountains was behind, but the T2 encountered clouds and rain and a strong side wind from the south. As night fell a violent thunderstorm with dazzling flashes of lightning swept over the prairies. To avoid the clouds the aviators flew very low and almost hit trees and farm-houses; they cleared these obstacles, however, being helped in steering their course by the lightning flashes that illuminated the landscape for miles around. It was a wild ride, for the storms they met were the fringes of a tornado, which did great damage to that section of country. The side wind made it difficult to keep to the course they had charted, but shortly before dawn they sighted the lights of St. Louis, and verified their reckonings again.

The T2 had now covered more than half of the distance from coast to coast and was flying easily, the load of gasoline being much lighter than on the first part of the journey. Daylight was a great aid and the plane skimmed along over level fields until some miles beyond Terre Haute the aviators discovered that the cylinder jackets were cracked and that water was squirting in small streams from both sides of the engine. They had noted one cracked cylinder when they were about four hundred miles out from San Diego, but that had not affected the running of the engine; now with twice as much water squirting out the plane could not keep in the air. Kelly poured the supply of beef broth and coffee into the radiator, and so cooled the engine that they were able to reach the Indianapolis Speedway before making a landing.

The first attempt to cross the continent had ended in the mountains near San Diego, the second attempt had brought the aviators as far as Indiana. Small wonder that this time they vowed they were through with transcontinental flights.

After a few days' rest, however, they began to make plans for another attempt, this time to fly from east to west, which they felt was the proper direction in which to try to cross the continent, providing the prevailing headwinds could be overcome. From the weather forecaster at Washington they learned that during the last two weeks of April each year there is a peculiar weather condition, known as a "Hudson Bay high," which reverses the usual wind direction across the continent and causes the wind to blow towards the west instead of towards the east.

They decided to wait until spring in order to take advantage of this, and meantime at McCook Field, in Dayton, Ohio, tried for new duration records. The record they had made above San Diego had not been accepted as official by the International Aeronautical Association, owing to some formality not having been complied with, and two Frenchmen held the record of 34 hours. Kelly and Macready made several attempts; the first time the wheels of their plane stuck in the mud and they could not get off the ground; the second time they flew for about eight hours when the engine got into trouble and they had to descend; on April seventeenth they rose into the air from the very place where the Wright brothers had made their first flights and Orville Wright himself acted as official observer for them. That time they stayed in the air just over 36 hours, and so won the world's duration record. Orville Wright had the satisfaction of seeing an airplane bearing a weight of 10,850 pounds remain aloft for a day and a half, and that only twenty years after the earliest few-minute flights of the crude biplane that he and his brother had invented.

The engine of the T2 was changed and the two aviators flew to Mitchel Field, on Long Island, where they prepared for the flight across country to the Pacific. The weather at first was not very promising, but on May first the Weather Bureau reported more favorable winds. As Mitchel Field was too small for a take-off with a heavy load the T2 was flown to the larger Roosevelt Field, where the gasoline tanks were filled. There, about noon on May 2, 1923, the plane, after two unsuccessful tries, rose from the ground and barely cleared the hangars, telegraph wires and trees. Such was the weight it carried that it moved slowly and only very gradually gained height as it flew over Long Island. It reached a better altitude—about 400 feet—as it crossed New Jersey and entered Pennsylvania. Then something happened to the ignition apparatus; the plane was flying entirely on the batteries and unless repairs could be made at once the aviators would be forced to land. Kelly made the necessary adjustments, a work difficult enough even on the ground in a repair shop, and the T2 went on. About dusk they reached Dayton, well ahead of schedule time.

West of Dayton clouds began to gather and the plane ran into a cold mist. On their first attempt at crossing the continent they had travelled against the light, now they were moving along with the darkness and this made the night much longer. From Indianapolis to Terre Haute they occasionally caught the lights of automobiles on a highroad; Terre Haute itself was only a glimmer seen through the fog. The moon had risen, but clouds hid its light entirely. Of St. Louis they caught only a faint glow, and then a steady rain began to fall. By the compass they steered to Jefferson City and there laid their course across five States toward Tucumcari, New Mexico.

The two aviators relieved each other as pilots every six hours. The active pilot sat in a small cockpit in the nose of the plane and when an exchange was to be made he slipped quickly out of his seat and the other slid into it. The relief pilot was constantly busy, checking the consumption of gasoline and oil, watching the engine and making what repairs were needed, and snatching a meal of sandwiches, broth, and coffee. Neither had any opportunity to sleep while in the air.

Soon after midnight the clouds gave way to bright moonlight and they were able to make their course without difficulty across the prairies of Kansas and Oklahoma. As the sun began to rise they came to New Mexico and saw below them Tucumcari, which, according to their schedule, they had planned to reach by dawn. Beyond this they flew into mountainous country and the hills ascended so steeply that the plane could hardly keep above them. At last they had to abandon the course they had mapped out and hunt for an opening through the mountains. They flew close to the top of a great forest until they saw what looked like a promising pass; this, however, instead of opening into a fertile valley, brought them into a series of canyons, so narrow as scarcely to allow room for turning about. Here they gave over seeking for the most favorable route and steered west by compass. This plan succeeded; they came to the sandy wastes of Arizona, then to the Colorado River, then to the wide, green fields of the Imperial Valley.

There was only one more range to cross and this the T2 surmounted easily. In the distance to the west the aviators could now descry the buildings of San Diego, which was their goal. They made a long swoop down from 8,000 feet and passed directly over the roofs, which were covered with people, looking for them. At 11.26 A. M. on May third, the T2 landed at Rockwell Field, having flown about 2,700 miles from Roosevelt Field, Long Island, in 26 hours 50 minutes, travelling at an average speed of about 100 miles an hour.

The continent had been crossed for the first time in a non-stop flight and congratulations flooded the successful aviators. One of the most interesting of the messages they received was signed "Ezra Meeker, New York"; this read: "Congratulations on your wonderful flight, which beats my time, made seventy-one years ago by ox-team. At two miles an hour, I was five months on the way. Happy to see, in my ninety-third year, so great a transformation in methods of travel. Ready to go with you next time."

The country from the Atlantic to the Pacific was successfully crossed in an airplane between dawn and dusk about a year after Macready and Kelly accomplished their great feat. The aviator who made this flight in one day was Lieutenant Russell L. Maugham, of the United States Air Service. Remarkable as this achievement was, it cannot fairly be compared with that of Macready and Kelly, for Maugham made his air-trip in six sections and de-

scended for fresh fuel at Dayton, St. Joseph, North
Platte, Cheyenne, and Salduro in Utah. His machine,
a Curtiss Pursuit model, only had to carry fuel sufficient for a flight of 600 miles and the pilot could
rest at each stopping place. On the other hand Lieutenant Maugham flew alone and at a much higher
rate of speed than Macready and Kelly. He left Mitchel Field, Long Island, on June 23, 1924, at 3 A. M.
(Eastern Standard time), and landed at 9.48 P. M.
(Pacific time) at Crissy Field, San Francisco. Only
17 hours 52 minutes were actually spent in the air,
so that Maugham's average speed for the 2700 miles
was more than 150 miles an hour, a very remarkable
record for a flight of such length.

CHAPTER XVI

AROUND THE WORLD

XVI

AROUND THE WORLD

WHEN successful long distance journeys had been made by airplane the aviators of various nations became ambitious to circumnavigate the globe. Flyers of England, France, Italy, Portugal, Argentina and the United States planned such an expedition; it was the United States that first accomplished it.

The American officers set about the work in a very thorough manner. They divided the route into seven sections, and each of these sections was put in charge of an advance officer, whose duty it was to make all arrangements for the assistance of the aviators in his sections: see to proper landing grounds, have mooring buoys in harbors, supply depots where stores, spare parts, and tools should be available.

After a study of various types of airplanes the Douglas Company of Santa Monica, California, was commissioned to build four planes which could be used over both land and water by the adoption of interchangeable wheeled undercarriages and pontoons. These machines were biplanes and each, when completely loaded and with its crew of two, would weigh something over four tons. Each plane could carry 465 gallons of gasoline, 30 gallons of oil, and

5 gallons of reserve water, and each was fitted with
a 450 horsepower, 12-cylinder, Liberty engine. A
sample Douglas Cruiser was given preliminary tests
in aerial flights at Dayton, Ohio, and was tested as a
seaplane at Hampton, Virginia.

The aviators of other countries had preferred the
eastward direction for making an around-the-world
journey, but the Americans chose the route westward. In this way they thought they would be able
to get across Alaska before the season of fogs, would
escape the typhoons of the China Sea and the mon-
soons of Burma and India, and fly over the North
Atlantic ahead of the Arctic winter.

The four planes were named for four cities on the
north, south, east, and west of the United States and
were christened the *Boston, New Orleans, Chicago,*
and *Seattle.* Major Frederick L. Martin was
commander-in-chief of the expedition, and with him
in the *Seattle* was Sergeant Alva Harvey. Aboard
the *Boston* were Leigh Wade and Henry H. Ogden;
on the *New Orleans* Erik H. Nelson and John Hard-
ing; on the *Chicago* Lowell H. Smith and Leslie P.
Arnold.

The planes started from Clover Field, Santa Monica, near Los Angeles, on March 17, 1924. The journey from here to Seattle, Washington, was to be regarded as a preliminary cruise to test the engines, as
the official flight was to commence from the latter
city. This journey was successfully made, and at Seattle the machines were tuned up and awaited the

word for the start. Early in the morning of April 6, 1924, the four machines, fitted with pontoons for the first part of the journey, rose into the air. They followed the Straits of Georgia, between Vancouver Island and the mainland; then on against headwinds and through sleet and snow until at five in the afternoon they arrived at Prince Rupert, which was their first stopping place.

In landing the *Seattle* made a sideslip, which broke some struts and wires, but these were easily repaired, and the journey was continued. They were heading now for Sitka, 300 miles to the north, and along the coast they encountered very thick fog. At Sitka they were stormbound for several days and here they replenished their supplies of gasoline and oil. Then on they went to Seward, passing through one snowstorm after another and having to lay their course by the intermittent glimpses they could catch of the rocky, mist-wreathed coast.

From Seward the route went to Chignik, which is a salmon cannery station on the Alaskan shore. Three of the planes reached this place, but the *Seattle* did not appear. Major Martin's machine had been forced down by a fracture of the crankcase, which let out the lubricating oil. He took shelter behind a headland, and the next day destroyers came to the rescue of the plane. Major Martin gave orders by wireless that a new engine should be sent from Dutch Harbor, the station on the Aleutian Islands, and directed the three other planes to continue to that station and wait for him there. On April nineteenth the *Boston, New Orleans,* and *Chicago* arrived at Dutch Harbor. Here new motors were installed on the three planes, as this was the last important station before crossing the North Pacific to Japan.

With the new engine the *Seattle* flew to Chignik on April twenty-fifth. Storms made travel impossible for three days, then more favorable weather reports led Major Martin to attempt to fly to Dutch Harbor. The plane was caught in a snowstorm and in trying to make a short cut across a promontory the pilot lost his way. Flying into a fog, he tried to climb out of it and ran his machine into a steep cliff with the result that the *Seattle* was wrecked beyond chance of repair.

The *Seattle* was now out of the competition and Major Martin and Sergeant Harvey were stranded in a fog in a mountainous and practically uninhabited country. They must find shelter and food before their emergency rations should be used up.

They started off to the south over the mountain that had wrecked the plane, but the fog was so thick that it seemed like part of the snow and prevented them from keeping to the course they intended. After floundering around for two hours they turned back to the crippled *Seattle* and made themselves as comfortable as they could by building a fire from the broken pieces of the machine. Then they climbed into the baggage compartment of the fuselage and tried to sleep, a difficult achievement with the roar of snowslides in the neighboring mountains.

The next morning the fog was as thick as on the day before, in fact the fog kept them where they were all that second day and second night. To supply fuel for their camp-fire they were obliged to chop up the plane's wings. They decided not to burn the fuselage, so when the fire went out they made a snow-house and managed to keep fairly warm.

On the third day the fog was still thick, but as provisions were running low they determined to attempt to make their way to some habitation. In order to keep on a straight course one went about a hundred yards ahead of the other, and if the one in front appeared to be moving out of line the other would check him up and shout directions.

Proceeding in this fashion, they were relieved when the fog lifted somewhat; doubly so when they discovered that they were within a few steps of a 1,500-foot precipice. Avoiding this, they reached by afternoon a level, marshy piece of ground, and here they camped by a thicket which furnished them with branches for a fire. They had left their fur-lined suits when they started out from the *Seattle,* because of the difficulty of tramping in them; now, clad only in their flying-clothes, they nearly froze. By morning they were both so nearly played out that they decided to turn back to the plane.

They reached it, but Sergeant Harvey's eyes were

almost blinded by the snow. In their first-aid kit there was boric acid and the use of this reduced the inflammation so that by the next day Harvey had nearly regained normal sight. They climbed the mountain and made out through their field-glasses a little lake to the southwest. Thinking that there might be a trapper's shelter there they started off, walked until four o'clock in the afternoon and made camp in a thicket of alders. There they were fortunately able to shoot two ptarmigan with a pistol, and on these they supped that night and breakfasted the next morning.

By noon they arrived at the lake, but there was no sign of any habitation on the shores. Consulting their hydrographic map they decided that their best plan would be to try to find a pass through the mountains somewhere to the south; the map showed that a stream might guide them to Ivanoff Bay.

There was a stream in the neighborhood and they followed it, but this stream flowed in the wrong direction. On they pressed, however, though they were nearly exhausted and Major Martin was now attacked by snow-blindness. Again they camped for the night; again by daylight they floundered on; another night was spent in the frozen wilderness, and the next day they came to a large stretch of water and saw a cabin. With feeble shouts they ran to it. Inside was a small supply of food, and also a small stove and a pile of wood. There they spent the most comfortable night since the wrecking of the plane.

Snow was falling thickly the next morning and continued all that day, that night, and the next day. On the morning of May ninth they attempted to locate their position and concluded that they were on Moller Bay, an arm of Bering Sea. With a rifle they found in the cabin they shot a couple of wild ducks and two snowshoe rabbits. The following morning they set out for Port Moller, which, according to the map, was at a distance of twenty-five miles from the cabin. The weather had now cleared and they made excellent progress. In the middle of the afternoon they spied a wireless mast and a smokestack. Then they saw a launch; the boat came towards them and they made out its occupants, two men and three women, natives of the coast. These people took Martin and Harvey aboard and ferried them across the water to a cannery building, where the superintendent and his men welcomed them warmly and sent word by radio that the missing aviators had safely arrived at Port Moller.

A few days later a cargo-boat carried the two across the North Pacific to Puget Sound, and from there they were able to reach Seattle.

In the meantime an official order had been sent on May second to the three airplane-crews at Dutch Harbor. This order appointed Lieutenant Lowell H. Smith commander of the expedition and directed him to push on with the three planes to Japan.

The next day therefore the *Chicago*, the *Boston*, and the *New Orleans* flew to Atka, an island some

400 miles west of Dutch Harbor. Stormy weather held them there several days; on the ninth they proceeded to the island of Attu, the most westerly of the Aleutian group and the last western outpost of North America.

While they waited at Attu for favorable weather the aviators received the news by wireless that Major Martin and Sergeant Harvey had reached safety.

If the reader will look at a map he will see that the Alaska Peninsula stretches out southwestward from the mainland of Alaska and that the Aleutian Islands, like a chain, carry the line of the peninsula part way across the southern section of Bering Sea. From the most western of these islands the next jump would be to the Komansdorski group of islands, which belong to Russia, then on to the eastern coast of Kamchatka, and from there to the Kurile Islands, which link Kamchatka with the north of Japan. The expedition had not received permission from the Soviet Government of Russia to land in their waters or territory, so when the planes reached Copper Island, one of the Komansdorski group, on May fifteenth, they had to alight outside the three-mile limit and close to the United States ship *Eider,* which was negotiating with the Soviet agents.

Word was brought next morning that the planes would not be allowed to land, but this did not interfere with the expedition's plans, and the planes set off on a 600-mile journey to Paramushiri in the Kuriles. They sighted Kamchatka and then, flying on through fog, rain and snow, reached Kashiwabara Bay, in Paramushiri, safely before noon. This was the first air voyage across the Pacific Ocean.

From there they went on to Tokio, which they reached on May twenty-fourth. Changing the engines and pontoons, they flew next across the sea to Shanghai, where they arrived on June fourth. Three days later they flew to Amoy, and then to Hongkong. The next flight was to Haiphong, in northern Annam; from there they continued down the coast for Tourane.

On this flight a cracked cylinder jacket forced the *Chicago* to land in a lagoon. The other planes alighted and then set off to Tourane for assistance. The *Chicago* was towed by native boats to Hué, a new engine was sent up from Saigon, and the airplane joined the *Boston* and *New Orleans* at Tourane on June fifteenth.

From Tourane the route of the three planes was to Saigon, Bangkok, Rangoon, and Akyab to Calcutta, in India. At Calcutta they changed the pontoons for the wheeled undercarriages, which were to be used until they reached the North Atlantic. When they arrived at Karachi they changed the engines of all three planes.

Bandar Abbas was reached on July seventh, Bagdad the next day, Aleppo the next, and Constantinople on July tenth. Across Europe they journeyed by Bucharest and Vienna to Paris. Then the Channel was crossed to the Croydon Air Port in England.

At Brough, near Hull, the machines were thoroughly overhauled and the pontoons fitted in place.

The flight was then resumed on July thirtieth to Kirkwall, in the Orkneys. At that place fog delayed the aviators several days, but on August second they started from Kirkwall for Hornafjord, in Iceland. Fog was encountered and when the *Boston* and the *Chicago* were clear of it they could not sight the *New Orleans*. These two planes returned to Kirkwall, and there that evening received a wireless message stating that the *New Orleans* had made its way through the fog to Hornafjord.

The two planes set out again; but engine trouble caused the *Boston* to descend south of the Faroes. The water was rough and the plane was considerably damaged. The *Chicago* flew off for aid, picked up the United States destroyer *Billingsby,* and this ship, together with the United States cruiser *Richmond,* steamed to the wrecked plane. An attempt was made to lift the *Boston* onto the cruiser's deck, but the tackle broke and the plane fell again in the sea. She was taken in tow, but the wind rose and the plane sank in the ocean when only about a mile from land.

The *Chicago* and the *New Orleans* continued the voyage from Hornafjord to Reykjavik on August fifth. Here they waited sixteen days for good weather and the establishment of supply depots on the coast of Greenland. An Italian aviator, Locatelli, with three companions, in a Dornier-Wal monoplane flying-boat was also planning to fly to Greenland, and accepted the invitation of the Americans to go with them.

August twenty-first they left Reykjavik. The Italian flew much the fastest and was soon out of sight of the others. They ran into fog and had several narrow escapes from icebergs, but succeeded in reaching Fredricksdal on the Greenland coast. American warships were sent to look for Locatelli and the flying-boat with its company was found floating on the water. In landing, however, the tail of the monoplane was injured and the boat was scuttled, so that it should not be a derelict in the way of ships.

At Ivigtut in Greenland new engines were installed in the two American planes and they started for Icy Tickle in Labrador. That place was reached on August 31, 1924, and the aviators were in North America again.

Southward they went by Newfoundland, Nova Scotia, New Brunswick, and Maine to Boston. At Pictou, in Nova Scotia, Lieutenants Wade and Ogden, of the wrecked plane *Boston,* joined them in a new machine, the *Boston II,* and continued with them.

Their triumphal journey westward across the continent took the aviators to New York, Washington, Dayton, Chicago, Dallas, El Paso, Los Angeles, San Francisco, and so to Seattle. This place from which they had started was reached at 1.28 P. M. (Pacific time) on September 28, 1924. The *Chicago* and the

New Orleans had flown around the world in a total flying time of 15 days, 3 hours, 7 minutes, a journey which had actually taken 175 calendar days. In the voyage 26,345 miles had been covered. The two airplanes and their crews had duplicated in the air what the sailors of Magellan's little ship *Victoria* had been the first to accomplish on the sea.

CHAPTER XVII

IN THE ARCTIC

XVII

IN THE ARCTIC

PICTURE an expanse of water and ice, reaching as far as the eye could see in any direction, not smooth like the desert but made up of blocks of ice standing on edge or piled on top of one another like toy building-blocks of giants, here and there a lead of open water, here and there a lead crammed with floating ice floes, mountains of ice that ground against each other, splintered and broke off, tearing holes in one part of the ice-pack and crunching fissures together in another.

Then picture down from the sky dropping a little flying-boat. It circles for a few minutes, as if undecided where to alight in such a jumbled waste, comes down in a small lagoon among the ice-floes, taxies over to a big ice-cake and stops there. Out climb three men, their eyes bloodshot, their legs unsteady, their ears almost deafened by the roar of the motor that has been whirring for hours. As they look about they catch sight of a seal that has popped his head up from the water; he stares a moment at the strange visitors that have come from the sky, then ducks under an ice-floe; they have that part of the world again to themselves.

It is one o'clock on the morning of May 22, 1925.

At 5 P. M. on the day before two Dornier-Wal flying-boats, the N 24 and the N 25, had left Kings Bay, Spitzbergen, to explore the Arctic and if possible reach the North Pole. Each of the boats had three men aboard; on the N 25 were Captain Roald Amundsen as navigator, Riiser-Larsen as pilot and Feucht as mechanic; on the N 24 were Lincoln Ellsworth, navigator, Dietrichson, pilot, and Omdal, mechanic. The two airships carried provisions to last for one month, allowing two pounds of food per day for each man.

The little expedition, of which Amundsen was the leader, had chosen the island of Spitzbergen as its base because of its situation, just halfway between Norway and the North Pole and only ten degrees or 600 nautical miles from the latter point. In addition an offshoot of the Gulf Stream sends a warm current along the western and northern shores of the island and thus produces ice-free waters at the highest latitude in the world. From April nineteenth to August twenty-fourth the sun never sets in the latitude of Kings Bay, and that is the season chosen for exploration.

The two flying-boats got a good start but presently ran into a thick bank of fog and had to rise to a height of 1,000 meters to clear it. Then as the mists disappeared the adventurers had a wonderful view of the Polar panorama, miles upon miles of snow and ice, glittering from many facets, a world of white, broken here and there by narrow cracks, or "leads," the only evidence of the continual movement of the gigantic pack. Over this expanse the airplanes winged at 75 miles an hour and so sped on for 8 hours until the sun had shifted from the west to a point directly ahead. The navigator's reckoning showed that they had travelled just six hundred miles and should now be above the North Pole, but a strong northeast wind had been blowing them to the west and so off their course. Their fuel was about half used up when they saw just ahead the first open lead of water large enough for a plane to land in that they had sighted on their journey. They decided to take advantage of this and descend to make observations and learn where they were. Captain Amundsen's airship—the N 25—circled for a landing; then his rear motor backfired and stopped, and the N 25 disappeared among some ice hummocks. The N 24 came down more successfully in the small lagoon and Ellsworth, Dietrichson and Omdal clambered out, were greeted by the seal, which promptly vanished, and then the three aviators took observations and found that their westerly drift had carried them 136 miles from the Pole.

Then they began to wonder what had happened to the N 25, and scrambling up on the highest neighboring hummocks they scoured the horizon with their field-glasses. Only ice and snow were to be seen, and it was not until they had scaled a particularly high hill about noon that they made out the other flying-boat, her nose pointing up at an angle of forty-five degrees, wedged against a thick cake of ice three miles away. The N 25 appeared to have crashed into a very rough piece of country.

The N 24 also was in some difficulties. At the take-off from Kings Bay the nails had been torn loose from the bottom of the plane and the machine was now leaking so badly that water was above the bottom of the gasoline tanks. The forward motor also was disabled, and as the three looked at their ship they asked themselves how they were ever going to get her up into the air again.

Omdal, the mechanic, set to work trying to repair the motor, while Ellsworth and Dietrichson attempted to get across country to the N 25. They took a canvas canoe which they had brought with them, hauled it up the hummocks and tumbled with it down into frozen crevasses. The ice was covered with snow to a depth of two or three feet. As they floundered along Dietrichson twice slipped down between the floes and was only able to keep from sinking below the ice by hanging on to the canoe. After going half a mile they were obliged to turn round and return to the lagoon.

Pitching their tent on top of the ice floe, they moved the equipment from the plane into it. They had plenty of work to do, Omdal busy with the motor and the other two taking turns at the pump in order to keep the water from rising above the gasoline tanks. They tied pieces of flannel to some small balloons, which they had taken along for the purpose of obtaining information about the upper air strata, and now set them loose, in the hope that the wind would blow them over towards the N 25 and so let the other party know where they were. The wind carried them in the wrong direction, however, or the balloons got entangled in the rough ice.

On the first day the wind blew from the north, but on the second it shifted to the south and the ice began to close in. By this time Amundsen had located the N 24 and as the two planes were drifting together the two parties were able to communicate with each other by semaphoring. On the third day Ellsworth and his companions made another attempt to reach Amundsen; putting their canvas canoe on a sledge they set off over the hummocks. This work was too tiring, and after going a few hundred yards they left the canoe and pushed on with their supplies packed on their backs.

A journey of two miles brought them to a large lead, which they saw no way to cross. They signaled to Amundsen and he advised them to return to their plane. Therefore, after ploughing for seven hours over hummocks and ridges, they turned back, reached their tent again, and cooked their supper of pemmican soup over the stove.

The hot soup, cups of coffee, and pipes of tobacco refreshed the three. Then Dietrichson exclaimed, "Something is the matter with my eyes." They had all been wearing snow-glasses, but Dietrichson had become snow-blind. The other two bandaged his eyes and put him to bed. Next day his eyes were better and he was able to share in the work.

That work consisted for the moment in getting the plane up on the ice floe, since it would be crushed if left in the lead. This was a difficult task, for they had only one wooden shovel and an ice-anchor to work with and with these had to loosen the snow and make a runway up which to haul the plane. Meantime, looking through their glasses, they could see that Amundsen had set the propellers of the N 25 going and was pulling up and down on the wings; his plane would not move, however, and presently he signaled the other party to come over and help in getting the N 25 out. Ellsworth had got the nose of his plane up on the ice, but as only one engine would work he could not get it higher. The plane was safe from sinking, but might be crushed if the ice pressed in against it. In the five days they had been there the ice had kept shifting, the heavy ice moving out, and by now the two planes were only half a mile apart. At Amundsen's signal therefore the crew of the N 24 loaded themselves up with packs of eighty pounds per man and began a journey across the freshly frozen leads, on new ice, to try to reach the others.

They felt their way as best they could over the crust of ice, shuffling along loosely on their skis, which they did not fasten firmly lest they should get tangled up if the wearers fell into the water. Omdal was ahead, followed by Ellsworth and Dietrichson. Suddenly Ellsworth heard a yell from Dietrichson, who was behind him, then Omdal in front also gave a yell and immediately disappeared through the thin ice. The crust under Ellsworth began to sag and he quickly jumped to one side, fortunately landing on some old thick ice which gave him secure footing. Lying down, he pushed his skis over towards Dietrichson and when the latter grabbed them Ellsworth was able to pull his floundering companion up to the firm ice. Then he turned to look for Omdal, and saw that only his head was above the water and that he was struggling to keep from going under by digging his fingers into the ice. Ellsworth reached him as he was on the point of going down and managed to hold him by the pack on his back until Dietrichson contrived to crawl over and grab him by the shoulders while Ellsworth cut off the heavy pack. It took all the strength of the two of them to pull Omdal up to safety.

The other party could not reach them nor even see them, as some very high hummocks rose directly in front of the N 25. Ellsworth and his two mates rested a while and then succeeded in getting over to Amundsen's camp, where they were supplied with dry clothes and hot chocolate. Both Omdal and Dietrichson had lost their skis in the water, a very serious loss since it seemed extremely probable that the whole party might have to attempt the four hundred mile journey to Greenland on foot.

The first business of the combined forces was to try to free the N 25 from her position. She was half on and half off an ice floe, her nose up on the ice and her tail down in the water. When the plane had landed she had floated in open water but now, owing to the constant shifting of the floes during the last five days, the N 25 was firmly locked in the ice. The six men set to work to build a slip up which they might haul the plane. A regular routine was now observed in the camp. Omdal was appointed cook and rations were apportioned. In that frozen world warmth was dearly prized, the morning and evening cup of chocolate, the noon cup of pemmican broth. Captain Amundsen said that the only times when they were really happy was when the hot chocolate was going down their throats and when they were rolled up in their reindeer sleeping bags.

The after-compartment of the N 25 became kitchen, dining-room and sleeping-quarters, a stuffy, draughty and uncomfortable place; the metal overhead was covered with hoarfrost and this turned into a steady drip as the heat from the stove warmed the cabin. Amundsen and Ellsworth slept in the pilot's cockpit, Riiser-Larsen in the tail, and the others in the after-compartment, where they stretched themselves on skis in order to keep off the metal bottom.

With three wooden shovels, a two-pound pocket safety-ax, an ice anchor, and sheath-knives lashed to the ends of ski-sticks, they constructed a slip and worked the N 25 up on the ice. The floe on which they were located measured 300 feet in diameter, and they needed a 400-meter course from which to take off in the plane. They would have preferred to take off in open water, but the wind was blowing steadily from the south and that did not open the water through the ice-pack.

On May twenty-eighth the N 25 was safely on the ice floe. The intention of the party had been to free the two planes and continue on their journey to the Pole; now, however, on account of the difficulties of their position, it seemed inadvisable to consider any other course but a return to Spitzbergen.

The next day Ellsworth, Omdal and Dietrichson made their way back to the N 24 with their canvas canoe and sledge. If the expedition was to get to Spitzbergen they must salvage the gasoline and provisions in that plane. They cut loose one of the empty tanks, filled it from one of the full ones, loaded it in the canoe, put the canoe and supplies on the sledge, and set out again. A large lead had in the meantime opened up behind them, and although they were able to get across this themselves they had to leave the sledge on the further side over night. By next morning the lead had closed up and so they succeeded in drawing the sledge with the gasoline and provisions to the camp by the N 25.

The party now took stock of supplies: they had 1,500 liters of fuel which allowed them a margin of 300 liters for the trip to Spitzbergen, if they were able to start immediately. They had also 285 half-pound cakes of pemmican, 300 cakes of chocolate,

42 condensed milk tins of malted milk tablets, 3 tins of oatmeal biscuits, 3 sacks of powdered milk, 3 sausages of 12 lbs. each, and 25 liters of kerosene for the stove.

With the object of working as long as possible to get the N 25 clear and also have sufficient provisions left with which to return to Spitzbergen Captain Amundsen cut down the daily rations to 300 grams per man, or just one half pound per man per day. In this way he estimated that their supplies would last for two months more.

Amundsen now set June fifteenth as the date on which they must make a definite decision as to what they should do. They must either start back on foot for Greenland on that date or stay by the plane with the hope of open water coming while the food diminished. Long they debated the two courses. Amundsen favored staying by the plane, arguing that with the arrival of summer the leads would open. Riiser-Larsen declared that he would start overland on foot on June fifteenth. Feucht voted for sticking by the N 25. Ellsworth preferred to wait until June fourteenth before making a decision. It was a long tramp to Greenland for men in a worn-out condition, carrying thirty pounds apiece on their backs, and dragging a canvas canoe with which to get across open leads.

By the end of May there were eight inches of ice in the lead on the far side of the floe where they had made their headquarters, and they decided to try a

DePinedo Flying from Italy to the American Continent

The Start of the London-Australian Flight

take-off from this new ice. Down to the lead was a
six-foot drop and to get the plane into position required two days' work at building a slip and leveling
off the ice for a distance of 500 meters. On June second they tried the slip; starting the motors, they
taxied across the floe and down the slip; but the slip
had too steep an elevation, and as the plane had not
sufficient speed it simply ploughed through the ice.
The motors were shut off and the crew settled down
to spend the night in the lead.

Amundsen awoke them at midnight by calling out
that the plane was being crushed. Immediately the
men got everything out onto the solid ice near by,
and worked the plane up and down so as to allow
the incoming ice to close in beneath the N 25 from
both sides. Luckily the plane was saved; it had almost been crushed like an egg-shell. With the morning came the first fog of the Polar summer season
and the temperature rose to freezing.

The crew continued the work of leveling a new
course, working over towards where the N 24 was
stranded, but there was not enough wind for the N 25
to rise in, and the plane kept breaking through the
surface of the thin ice. The N 25 was also leaking
from the pressure of the ice cakes, and Amundsen
and Ellsworth pitched their tent on the floe by the
N 24, which had now listed sideways in such a position that the tip of one wing was tightly fastened in
the newly frozen ice-pack. The ice, freezing in from
both sides, had made a long, narrow lane in front

of the N 24, but this lane curved in places. However, Riiser-Larsen thought that there was a possibility of getting a take-off here, so he started the N 25 and taxied forward. When he slowed up to go around a curve the nose of the plane broke through the ice and the N 25 abruptly halted, lifting its tail in the air. The others jumped out and cut the ice away so that the plane could settle on an even keel.

The ice-pack was hemming them in and they could not stay where they were, so they started to make an extension of the course, a gigantic task, as the ice was covered with frozen lumps and ridges. For two nights and a day they labored with their makeshift tools. Then, when they looked on the morning of June fifth at the track they had worked so hard to clear they saw that it was a mass of tumbled ice blocks.

If they were to get away aboard one of the planes they must find a floe of sufficient size to furnish them with a take-off. Next morning Riiser-Larsen and Omdal set off in a heavy fog to see if they could find such a floe. They were gone all day, but at nightfall returned with news that they had discovered a floe that they thought would serve the purpose. It was half a mile from camp, and to reach it they would have to build a slip and bridge two ice cakes.

An ice wall was moving up in the rear of the N 25. The motors were started and the position of the plane was shifted; within fifteen minutes solid ice had closed in over the place where it had been. Then work began on building the slip; after six hours it was constructed and the plane was safely up on floe No. 1. Next day they started the biggest job they had yet tackled; to cut a passage through a ridge of ice fifteen feet thick that separated floe No. 1 from floe No. 2, and then to bridge a chasm fifteen feet wide and ten feet deep between the two floes. This work they succeeded in accomplishing, though they had to labor at top speed lest the floes should drift apart while they were bridging them. They arrived on the big floe and in order to take advantage of the south wind immediately leveled a track across the shortest diameter of the ice, which would give the plane about 300 meters for a take-off. Before they had finished making the track the wind died down, but they made a try at flying; the plane only bumped along and came to a halt just in front of an open lead.

On June ninth they began to construct a new course for a take-off, and succeed they must this time they felt if they were ever to get away, for the southerly winds were making the snow too soft to travel over and the leads would not open in the constantly shifting ice. The task was to remove two and a half feet of snow down to solid ice and level a track twelve meters wide and four hundred meters long. The snow must also be thrown six meters clear on each side, so as to allow room for the wing stretch of the plane.

The new course was completed on June fourteenth. Riiser-Larsen paced it off and found that instead of

four hundred meters it measured five hundred.
Amundsen thereupon declared that a million dollars
couldn't buy that extra hundred meters from him;
it would be of priceless value in trying to lift the
plane.

That evening they decided to make an attempt at
flight; the wind was from the south and of no assistance on this course; the plane only bumped forward
and would not rise. For a successful take-off they
needed to get off with a speed of 100 kilometers per
hour and the best they had previously done was 40
kilometers. At this attempt, however, they had made
60, which was a decided improvement.

The wind shifted in the night from the south to
the north; it was the second time during their
twenty-five days in the ice that the wind had blown
from that quarter. The surface of the snow was crisp
and hard. The day was June fifteenth, the date on
which they had decided either to attempt a flight
or try to tramp overland to Spitzbergen. They
dumped out of the plane everything they could
spare: one of the canvas canoes, rifles, cameras, field-
glasses, and even their sealskin parkas and heavy
ski-boots, which they replaced with moccasins. Of
their supplies they only kept half of the food, one
canvas canoe, a shotgun and one hundred pounds of
ammunition.

All the party climbed into the N 25 and Riiser-
Larsen started the engine. Dietrichson was the navigator. The plane moved, bumped along for four hun-

dred meters, and then, in that last priceless hundred meters, lifted from the track. They were off, they were in the air; the N 25 was winging southward!

Through a thick fog they flew for two hours, setting their course by a magnetic compass. As frequently as he could Dietrichson dipped to secure drift observations, but the fog hung so low that he had to fly close to the ice, in one place skimming it at a height of only one hundred feet. At last they rose above the fog, and navigation became an easier matter. Southward they flew and after six hours of steady going Feucht shouted, "Land!"

This land did not appear to be Spitzbergen; it might be Franz-Josefs-Land. It was land, however, and a cheering sight. They did not have to stick to their rationing regulations and began to munch the chocolate and biscuits from their scanty store.

The stabilization rudders were becoming more and more difficult to manage and presently the N 25 was obliged to come down on the open sea, just after it had passed the edge of the Polar pack. After flying for eight hours the plane landed in the water; there were barely ninety liters of gasoline in the tanks, one half hour's fuel supply. So rough was the water that the aviators had to go below and cover up the man-holes, as the waves were breaking over the plane.

Through that choppy sea they taxied some distance and then reached the land. Mooring the plane to a large piece of ice, the men went ashore, thankful to have gained a haven that was solid earth, not shifting floes. They heard birds singing, a little stream ran between the rocks on the beach, there was plenty of driftwood for use in bonfires if they wanted them. They ate supper and took observations with the sextant; these showed then that they were at Nord Kap on Nordostland, the very point for which they had been steering all day. Then Riiser-Larsen cried, "There is a ship!" To the east, around a headland, glided a little cutter.

The cutter changed her course as if the men aboard had not seen those on shore. Instantly Amundsen's party packed their supplies again on the plane, started the motor, and whizzed over the sea in pursuit of the ship. The N 25 came up alongside the cutter—which was the *Sjöliv* of Balsfjord, commanded by Captain Nils Wollan—and a boat was lowered and two men rowed out to the plane. The aviators were taken aboard the ship and a tow-rope attached to the N 25.

On the cutter they had a royal feast while the vessel set out for Kings Bay. A headwind made it difficult, however, to tow the plane, so the next morning they beached the N 25 in Brandy Bay, North Cape, North-East-Land, Spitzbergen. They would go on to Kings Bay for assistance and fresh supplies, and then return for the seaplane and fly it to harbor.

For three days they voyaged in the *Sjöliv*, which had been hunting seals. Ellsworth said: "We slept continuously during the three days in the sealer, only waking to devour the delicious seal meat steaks smothered in onions and the eider-duck egg omelets prepared for us.''

At Kings Bay they arrived safely and several days later a ship brought the N 25 back from Brandy Bay. On June twenty-fifth Amundsen's party put the plane aboard a steamer bound for Norway, and nine days later they reached the Norwegian Naval Base at Horten, near Oslo. Then, on July fifth, the hardy adventurers flew the good N 25 into Oslo to be welcomed by great cheering throngs.

After all the difficulties they had encountered since they had first come down in the Polar ice-pack it was little short of a miracle that they had been able to make a successful take-off in the N 25 and voyage through the fogs of the Arctic Ocean back to the shores of Europe in their staunch little seaplane.

CHAPTER XVIII

IN THE WAKE OF COLUMBUS

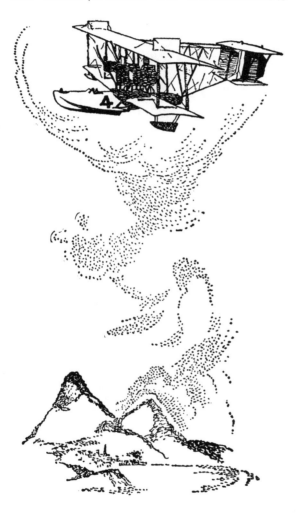

XVIII

IN THE WAKE OF COLUMBUS

ON August 3, 1492 Christopher Columbus sailed from the port of Palos, in Spain, on board the little ship *Santa Maria,* in company with two other vessels, the *Pinta* and the *Niña.* His aim was to reach the northern part of Cipango, or Japan, which, according to his map, appeared to be on the direct route to the wonderfully rich cities of Cathay that had been described by the great traveller Marco Polo. Sailing west for many days, Columbus and his men sighted a long low shore on October 12, 1492 (according to the "new style" of the Gregorian Calendar, October 21, 1492), and there landed. This shore was actually one of the Bahama Islands; and instead of finding Cipango Columbus had discovered that great western world that was afterwards known as North and South America.

Some four hundred and thirty-four years later, on January 22, 1926, a Dornier-Wal flying-boat, christened the *Ne Plus Ultra,* was floating in the harbor of Palos, ready to start on a voyage through the air from Spain to South America by way of the Canary and the Cape Verde Islands. The crew of the flying-boat consisted of Major Franco of the

Spanish Army, Captain Ruiz de Alda, Lieutenant Duran, and an experienced mechanic.

The plan of the voyage was to fly from Spain to the Canary Islands, a distance of 812 miles; from there to the Cape Verde Islands, a distance of 1060 miles; and then to Pernambuco, in Brazil, a distance of 1,777 miles. The goal the aviators hoped to reach in the western hemisphere was Buenos Aires, in Argentina, which would make a total air journey of 6,259 miles. Two Portuguese aviators, Commanders Cabral and Coutinho, had flown in the previous year from Lisbon to Pernambuco by way of Las Palmas, St. Vincent, and St. Paul's Rocks. At the last named place their seaplane had been wrecked and they had had to wait until a new plane could reach them by ship. They had succeeded in reaching South America at Pernambuco, but because of the accident to the machine the voyage had actually taken more than two months.

There was great excitement in Palos when at eight o'clock in the morning the *Ne Plus Ultra* rose from the water on January twenty-second. Circling the monument to Columbus, the flying-boat set off to the south. At four o'clock that afternoon the aviators reached the Canary Islands. There they waited a few days, then, with a somewhat lighter load, took off from Gando Bay, Grand Canary, on the second "hop" of the voyage.

The flying-boat winged on its way without mishap and in the evening of the day on which it had started arrived at the Cape Verde Islands, having made a journey of more than 1,000 miles since morning. On January thirtieth the aviators started to fly across the Atlantic to South America, by far the longest "hop" of the expedition.

All went well until the *Ne Plus Ultra* came to the waters off the Fernando Noronha Islands, which are situated some 300 miles from Pernambuco. There darkness came on the sea and the flying-boat was obliged to descend. Ships towed the machine safely to harbor, and the next day the flight was continued to Pernambuco, where the Brazilians welcomed the Spanish aviators with the greatest enthusiasm.

The air voyage from Pernambuco to Rio de Janeiro, a distance of 1,260 miles, was made on February fourth. On February ninth the *Ne Plus Ultra* flew 1,200 miles to Montevideo, and on the following day arrived early in the afternoon at Buenos Aires. Argentine aircraft went to meet the Spaniards and escorted the flying men in triumph to their destination in the port.

This great flight from Palos, in Spain, to Buenos Aires, in the Argentine, had been made in a total journey, including waits, of twenty days. The most remarkable feature of this air trip from Europe to South America was the long distance of the successive flights in which it had been made, 812, 1,060, 1,450, 300, 1,260, 1,200 and 150 miles. On no other flight of equal length had aviators achieved so many long distance jumps.

CHAPTER XIX

TO THE NORTH POLE

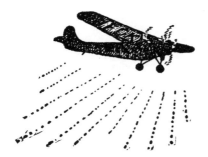

XIX

TO THE NORTH POLE

MANY aviators had sought to fly over the North Pole since its discovery by Peary in 1909, but various accidents had befallen the expeditions until 1926. In the spring of that year an airplane, flown by Lieutenant-Commander Richard E. Byrd and his mechanic Floyd Bennett, reached the coveted goal, and in less than twenty-four hours after Byrd's plane had returned to its base the news was received by wireless that a dirigible, flown by Captain Roald Amundsen, Lincoln Ellsworth, and Colonet Umberto Nobile, was also flying over the Pole.

Byrd's machine was a commercial three-engined Fokker, which the aviator had christened the *Josephine Ford,* in honor of the daughter of Edsel Ford, since Edsel Ford had contributed to the funds for the expedition. In this monoplane Byrd and Bennett took off from Kings Bay, Spitzbergen, on May 9, 1926, at 12.30 A. M. (Greenwich time). The sun was shining, there were no headwinds, and not a wisp of fog was to be seen. A course was laid as straight as possible to the North Pole.

They gained altitude gradually and presently were flying two thousand feet above the water. The two aviators alternated at the wheel, each steering for two hours at a time. Their object was to make a beeline and to this they stuck. After several hours of flying they became hungry and drank hot tea from their thermos bottles. Then Byrd found an oil leak in the right-hand motor and asked Bennett to investigate it. Bennett did so and thought that it might be best for them to land and try to repair the leak. They were at the time, however, within an hour's flight of the Pole, and therefore Byrd decided to fly on, and to check the leak he throttled down the starboard motor.

For an hour they sped; then Byrd made fresh calculations and discovered that they were above the Pole. They had reached their goal at the time they had figured, at 9.04 A. M. (Greenwich time), on May tenth. The aviators shook hands; sent the plane ahead several miles, then circled and flew back over the ribbed ice about the Pole and took some photographs of the neighborhood.

The question now was: what should they do about the leaky oil tank on the return journey? Bennett favored making a landing, if possible, to attempt repairs. Byrd again favored flying rather than trying to descend. At length they set their course for Gray Hook, Spitzbergen.

The wind now freshened and soon they were flying at more than a hundred miles an hour. The only sound in that desolate region was the roar of the machine's motors. At the great speed they were making it was only three hours after leaving the Pole that they were again in the area of explored territory.

Amundsen and Ellsworth and Nobile were at supper about six of that afternoon when the word was cried through the harbor of Kings Bay that "Byrd is coming!" The three aviators looked and saw the monoplane a tiny speck in the sky. It drew nearer, flew above the port, then swooped downward and lightly landed.

Byrd had reached the long-sought goal and come safely back, to be welcomed most generously by his friendly rivals.

Amundsen and his companions were planning to fly to the Pole in the *Norge,* a new and very fine dirigible built in Italy. Colonel Umberto Nobile had built this airship himself and because of his familiarity with every part of it he had been selected to be its pilot. On April 10, 1926, the *Norge* had started from Rome for Toulon, France, and from there had flown to Pulham, England, to Oslo, Norway, and to Leningrad, Russia. At Leningrad the dirigible was overhauled, and then proceeded to Kings Bay, Spitzbergen, where she arrived early in May. On May tenth the three aviators, Amundsen, Ellsworth, and Nobile, announced to the crew of the dirigible that, weather permitting, they proposed to start for the Pole the next day.

The *Norge* carried sufficient fuel in her tanks to give her a cruising range of some 2,700 miles, and the plan was to sail her across the North Pole region from Kings Bay, Spitzbergen, to Point Barrow, Alaska, a distance of 2,000 miles, and from Point Barrow to Nome, where there were excellent landing facilities.

As it happened, Byrd and Bennett had reached the Pole that day, May tenth, and had returned to Kings Bay to be hailed as the first to fly over the northern goal. That evening Byrd and Bennett celebrated their success with Amundsen, Ellsworth, Nobile, and Lieutenant Riiser-Larsen of the *Norge* expedition. The next morning, May eleventh, at 9 A. M. (Greenwich time), the dirigible started north from Kings Bay.

The *Norge* made good time and in less than two hours was north of Danes Island. The weather was fine, and the airship, flying at a height of about 1,400 feet, was making almost 64 miles an hour. Over the ice-pack she drew north steadily; no land was visible, only the great domain of ice, moving here and there. All that day the *Norge* flew easily; at 6.30 P. M. she was moving at a speed of about 52 miles an hour; Nobile was propelling her with only the left engine and allowing the right engine to rest. Later he alternated with the other engine.

Then a headwind commenced to blow and by midnight the *Norge* was sailing at a height of not much over 650 feet. Fog now blew above the airship and hid the sun and sky. The fog later scattered and when the airship was in the neighborhood of the

Commander Richard E. Byrd flying over the North Pole in
his Monoplane

Pole the aviators had a view of the ice below them. Calculations of position were made, and at 2.30 A. M. on May twelfth it was discovered that the *Norge* was above the North Pole. The airship was allowed to descend, and Amundsen, Ellsworth, and Nobile dropped flags of their respective countries attached to steel-pointed rods that stuck upright in the ice.

The *Norge* circled twice about the flags, then set off for Point Barrow, Alaska. Up to this time news of her flight had been sent broadcast by a powerful Marconi wireless outfit, but now moisture was freezing on the wireless antenna and soon after leaving the North Pole the Marconi outfit was unable to send messages or receive them. The party had the satisfaction of knowing, however, that they had sent the first message ever despatched from the North Pole.

Onward the *Norge* forged across a waste of ice that had never been explored. The course of the airship was constantly checked by the radio goniometer and by longitude observations of the sun. At 7 A. M. the Ice Pole or Pole of Inaccessibility, as it is also called—the centre of the Polar ice-pack, lying about 400 miles south of the North Pole—was reached. Then the airship ran into a dense fog and had to proceed slowly. Ice formed on various parts of the dirigible. But presently conditions became better and the sun, seen from time to time, allowed of the making of observations. At 8.15 A. M. the first land was sighted since they had left Kings Bay. It was Point Barrow, Alaska, the goal they had been making for.

To avoid running into the mountains of Alaska, Nobile set the course out over Bering Sea. Presently the direction was altered and the *Norge* headed for Cape Prince of Wales. Now a storm blew up and made it extremely difficult to choose a landing place. For twenty-five hours the *Norge* roved above the coast of Alaska, then the aviators sighted the little settlement of Teller, not far to the north of Nome.

The dirigible circled above Teller, then one of the crew slid down the anchor rope and fastened the airship to the ice of Grandley Harbor. The party landed, and as soon as the wireless outfit could be repaired the news was sent to Nome and from Nome to the outside world that the *Norge* had flown across the North Pole in a single flight from Spitzbergen to Alaska.

Amundsen, Ellsworth, and Captain Wisting left Teller on the next day for Nome while the others of the expedition demounted the airship and packed it to be sent to Seattle.

So it was that Byrd's monoplane and the dirigible of the Amundsen-Ellsworth-Nobile party each flew over the North Pole and returned successfully.

CHAPTER XX

LINDBERGH

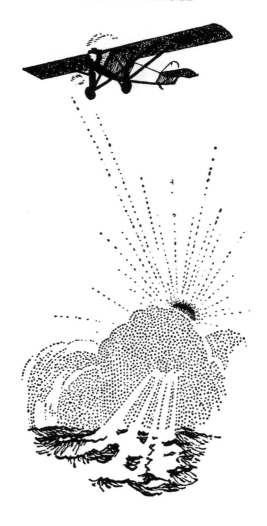

XX

LINDBERGH

A YOUNG American rose in an airplane from Roosevelt Field, Long Island, New York, at 7.52 A. M. on May 20, 1927, flew across the North Atlantic Ocean, and thirty-three hours later landed safely at Le Bourget, outside Paris, the capital of France. The Atlantic Ocean had already been successfully crossed in an airplane by Alcock and Brown, who had flown from Newfoundland to Ireland in 1919. How did it happen that the American aviator, Charles A. Lindbergh, by his flight from New York to Paris won the greatest applause ever accorded to a flying man and became one of the greatest popular heroes in history?

There were a number of reasons for this, and two are outstanding: Lindbergh flew alone, entirely dependent on his own skill and courage; Lindbergh's personality, modest and unassuming, won the admiration and affection of all who came in contact with him and that admiration and affection was by them transmitted to the rest of the world. He personified fearless, unselfish youth, and so drew all hearts to him; men saw in him the ideal adventurer, dauntless, chivalrous, a man of the highest character.

Such men as he knit the nations together in friendship and esteem and Lindbergh has become America's ambassador of good will to peoples in many quarters of the globe.

Soon after Byrd and Amundsen had succeeded in flying to the North Pole in the spring of 1926 Raymond Orteig, who had been a resident of the United States and was now a Paris hotel owner, offered a prize of $25,000 to the airplane crew who should make the first non-stop flight from Paris to New York, or from New York to Paris. Aviators of France and the United States engaged in friendly rivalry to win the prize. Captain René Fonck, of France, was the first to make the attempt, but his plane was wrecked as it took off from Roosevelt Field. During the winter of 1926–27 a number of planes were built in the United States to compete for the Orteig award; one of these was constructed at Los Angeles for a young air mail pilot, by the name of Charles A. Lindbergh, nicknamed "Slim" by his friends.

This aviator, a tall, handsome, blue-eyed fellow, had been born in Detroit in 1902. The Lindbergh family had moved to Little Falls, Minnesota, and the father had been elected a member of the United States House of Representatives. Young Charles went to the University of Wisconsin and took the course in mechanical engineering. Fascinated by the science of aviation he then went to a flying school at Lincoln, Nebraska. In 1925 he was graduated as a pilot at the Army Aviation School at San Antonio,

Texas. Having shown remarkable ability as an aviator, he had no difficulty in obtaining desirable positions; first with the Mile-Hi Airways Company, at Denver, Colorado, and then with the Robertson Aircraft Corporation, of St. Louis, which held a contract from the government to carry air mail between St. Louis and Chicago.

As chief pilot of the air mail he had many wonderful experiences in flying in all kinds of weather and was so successful in his trips that his associates dubbed him "Lucky" Lindbergh. While he was in the air mail service he obtained a captaincy in the 110th Observation Squadron of the Missouri National Guard. Then came the announcement of the Orteig prize and Lindbergh decided that he would try to win it if he could get a proper plane.

Through the friendly aid of Harold Bixby, of St. Louis, a business man much interested in aviation, a number of St. Louis citizens supplemented the fund that Lindbergh had saved from his earnings and thus enabled him to set about the purchase of a plane. He investigated various types of machines and decided that the one best suited for his purpose was a monoplane with a single motor. The monoplane he considered more serviceable than the biplane because of the lack of interference between the wings, which enabled it to carry a greater load for each square foot of surface at a higher speed. The single-motored machine had much less head resistance and therefore possessed a greater cruising range.

Lindbergh therefore placed an order for such a machine with the Ryan Airlines, of San Diego, California. The plane was to be equipped with a Wright Whirlwind 200 horsepower radial air-cooled motor. It also was to have a small cabin to protect the pilot from storms, with a periscope for vision ahead and side windows for looking right and left. He watched the building of the plane and when it was completed found that it flew perfectly on its first test flight. In compliment to the men who had helped him to buy the plane he christened it the *Spirit of St. Louis.*

A number of accidents occurred that spring to aviators who were planning to compete for the Orteig prize. In April Lieutenant-Commander Noel Davis and Lieutenant S. H. Wooster were killed when their biplane *American Legion* crashed to earth in Virginia. The Fokker monoplane *America,* built specially for the flight across the Atlantic, was wrecked in New Jersey and its captain, Lieutenant-Commander Richard E. Byrd, and its pilot, Floyd Bennett, together with two others of the crew, were injured. In May, Lindbergh heard that the celebrated French war Ace, Captain Charles Nungesser, and Major François Coli, were preparing at Le Bourget Flying Field, outside Paris, to take off for New York. On May seventh the two French aviators started; storms were encountered; and although search was made of their route across the water and of lands where they might have landed no trace was discovered of them or their plane.

Commander Byrd's Plane in Which He Flew from New
York to the Coast of France

First Successful Flight from San Francisco to Honolulu

Meantime at Long Island Clarence D. Chamberlin was waiting for news of the French aviators before making his start. Richard E. Byrd was also working on his plane in preparation for the transatlantic flight. Then arrived Lindbergh in the *Spirit of St. Louis.* He had made the journey from San Diego to St. Louis in a single flight and from there had sped to Roosevelt Field. He reached that place on the afternoon of May twelfth. Little was known about him as an aviator; he was said to be a skillful and daring Western air mail pilot. To those who greeted him he said that he intended to try to fly from Roosevelt Field to Paris.

"Who's going with you?" he was asked.

"Nobody," was his smiling answer.

The weather was unsuitable for flying; there were either fogs or strong winds. At Roosevelt Field were now gathered the crew of Chamberlin's monoplane *Columbia,* the crew of Byrd's monoplane *America,* and Lindbergh with his monoplane *Spirit of St. Louis.* On the morning of May nineteenth the sky was cloudy and a light rain was falling. That evening Lindbergh received a report from the New York Weather Bureau stating that there was a high pressure area over the entire North Atlantic and that the low pressure over Nova Scotia and Newfoundland was receding. The moon had just passed full and conditions seemed to be favorable for a transatlantic flight.

Lindbergh told his mechanics to make the plane

ready for service and went to his hotel for a little rest. When he reached the field the next morning before daylight a light rain was falling and this continued until about dawn. The plane was at Curtiss Field, which adjoined Roosevelt Field, and moving to the latter place took some time, so that it was nearly eight o'clock before everything was ready for the start. At 7.52 A. M. the *Spirit of St. Louis* left the ground, gathered speed slowly, cleared some high trees, and took a compass course over Long Island Sound.

For food Lindbergh took with him a packet of sandwiches and seven days' emergency army fare; two canteens of water hung in the cockpit near his seat. Alone, he was to pilot his plane for a day, a night, and a day.

At first there was haze above the water, but from Cape Cod to Nova Scotia the weather was clear and he flew very low, sometimes at a height of only ten feet. Crossing Nova Scotia he ran into a stormy tract and flew through several cloudbursts. He saw the ocean covered with ice cakes and passed many icebergs after he left the Newfoundland coast.

He made the flight from New York to St. Johns in twelve hours, as he had estimated, and got his last glimpse of the continent of North America at four o'clock in the afternoon (New York time) when he flew over Main-a-dieu, Cape Breton. He steered now straight across the ocean. By eight in the evening it was dark; a fog had risen from the water;

there was no moon and he could only see a few indistinct stars. Below he made out great icebergs. Clouds blew up and hindered his vision ahead and to the sides. The air grew colder; sleet started to collect on the plane, and to avoid this he made several detours in an effort to reach clearer air.

After about two hours of flying in darkness the moon rose above the horizon and navigation became less difficult.

Other aviators had thought that the greatest danger in making such a long flight alone was that the pilot would become drowsy and fall asleep while steering the plane. Lindbergh did not have the difficulty in keeping awake that many expected; the weather was his greatest obstacle; in the storm he had to rely on his own instinct, the experience he had gained from flying in all sorts of atmospheric conditions as an air mail pilot, and the dials of his instruments, for much of the time he could see neither sky nor water.

Dawn came, the storm decreased and in the warmer atmosphere there was less likelihood of sleet coating the plane. When the sun rose Lindbergh could see through the fog and descended to a height of a hundred feet above the water. Presently the clouds floated higher and the plane rose with them. During the morning the weather kept on clearing and the aviator had a picture of the white-capped waves of the ocean far below him.

In that ocean he saw porpoises and some birds

skimming above the waves. Then in the afternoon he sighted a small fishing-boat and presently a fleet of them. Circling lower until he was within a few feet of one of the boats, he called out: "Which way is Ireland?" The fishermen probably did not understand the question; if they shouted back an answer, Lindbergh did not catch it as the plane flew on.

Within an hour he made out a rugged coastline to the northeast and judged that it was not more than ten or fifteen miles distant. This land he took to be the southwestern part of Ireland, and in order to verify the correctness of this supposition he changed his course and flew towards the nearest shore. The land was Ireland; flying low, he was able to locate Cape Valentia and Dingle Bay.

When he left Ireland he saw a number of steamers and sailing-ships. In two hours he was above the coast of England. Still flying low, he passed the southern counties and the port of Plymouth. Rising again, he sped above the English Channel and passed over Cherbourg in France. The weather was clear now and he could see the landscape for miles in all directions.

The sun was setting as he steered his plane towards the Seine and soon he could distinguish the beacons along the airway from London to Paris. The lights of the French capital became visible shortly before 10 P. M. (5 P. M. New York time). Rockets blazed up from the city to direct him and a great row of vertical lights showed him the outline of the Eiffel Tower.

He could see the lights of Le Bourget Flying Field, but thinking that the goal he sought was farther from the city he went on to the northeast for several miles to see if there was not another landing place that might be Le Bourget. Not finding such a field, he turned and circled down to the lights he had first seen. Below him was a sea of beacons, he had a glimpse of long lines of hangars, roads filled with automobiles and crowded with people.

Flying low over the field, he circled around into the wind, and made a successful landing. When the machine stopped rolling he turned it and started to taxi in the direction of the flaring beacons. The field was covered with an immense throng running towards the plane. To avoid injuring the crowd with the circling propeller Lindbergh cut the switch; to prevent the plane from being wrecked by the pressure of the multitude he climbed out of the cockpit with the intention of organizing a guard. There was such an uproar his shouts could not be heard. As he stepped from the plane he was caught up by the welcoming throng and carried on its shoulders in a triumphant march. From these strenuous admirers he was presently rescued and managed to find refuge in one of the hangars while French soldiers and police contrived to surround the plane and safeguard it from a multitude of souvenir-hunters.

People in far-off countries had followed that flight with breathless interest and all the world joined in the welcome of France to the young American who had flown alone from New York to Paris and had covered approximately 3,600 miles in 33 hours. The American Ambassador to France, Myron T. Herrick, took Lindbergh to his home, and from there, after a rest, the hero went on a tour that was a series of remarkable plaudits.

To make such a flight as Lindbergh's, to start on an air journey across the ocean alone, to fight through fog and storm in the night with wild waters beneath, to have the courage and nerve to fly on and on,— these are tests of the heroic in man. Lindbergh was a hero. He was also more than that, as he showed when he had succeeded in accomplishing his purpose and received the honors the world richly heaped on him. He was a gentleman of rare modesty and courtesy. With the world at his feet he was the same charming, simple, unassuming youth he had been in the days when he had piloted the air mail between St. Louis and Chicago.

Therein lies the keynote of his triumph, of the affection that people of all lands have shown for him. The world loves a hero, but sometimes under the gold of heroism it discovers the dross of selfishness. There was no dross in this hero. As people came to meet Lindbergh and know him better they found that he was unspoiled by his great triumph, that he sought neither fame nor wealth, that his purpose simply was, as he himself put it, "to advance aviation."

He did much more than advance aviation, he was the envoy of good will among races. When the French people cheered him at Le Bourget and in the streets of Paris they were expressing an affection for a messenger of friendship from America, one who had come to strengthen the bonds between the lands of Washington and Lafayette. He represented an ideal; to them he was an embodiment of the brotherhood of nations.

Lindbergh spent a week in Paris and delighted the French, from the President of the Republic to the children he smiled at in the streets; he called upon Louis Blériot, the man who had first flown across the English Channel; then he flew to Brussels, where the King and Queen of Belgium welcomed him. From Brussels he continued his journey through the air to Croydon Field, on the outskirts of London. The King and Queen of England received him and the English people added their acclaim to the honors done him by their government. He returned to Paris, and on June fifth took off for Cherbourg in his machine, accompanied by twenty airplanes. From Cherbourg he sailed on the United States ship *Memphis,* which had been placed at his service by President Coolidge for the voyage home.

He reached Washington on June eleventh. His mother was the first to embrace him; then came receptions by the President and other national officials. New York accorded him a wonderful welcome, and Raymond Orteig presented him with the prize for his New York-to-Paris flight. St. Louis greeted him next, and then Lindbergh was allowed to rest on his laurels.

Presently he flew again, over all sections of the United States. To Mexico and the countries of Central America he brought greetings from the air and was hailed by all these peoples as an envoy of friendship. His ready smile, his simple speech made him at home everywhere. As the *Spirit of St. Louis* had won its way over the stormy Atlantic, so the personality of its pilot won its way to the affections of men.

A great aviator, and a modest, sincere gentleman— so has the world acclaimed Charles A. Lindbergh.

CHAPTER XXI

THE NEW ERA

XXI

THE NEW ERA

I

WHAT a wonderful achievement it is—this ability to fly through the air as on the wings of a bird! Men have always wanted to be able to imitate "the way of an eagle in the air" and the fascination of voyaging above the world on winged horses or magic carpets is shown in the legends and folk stories of all countries. Shepherds of the ancient world watched the birds and wondered how it was that they sustained themselves in air, scholars of Europe in the Renaissance and afterwards, pondered the problem, drew diagrams and wrote learned treatises about it. Yet not until near the end of the eighteenth century did men—so far as we know—actually succeed in voyaging through the air.

When they did first succeed in so voyaging it was not in a machine with wings like those of a bird, not in a machine heavier than the air, but in the lighter-than-air balloon. The Montgolfières, or fire-balloons, and the gas-balloons of Charles and others, enabled aviators to float above the clouds and inaugurated the first era of practical aeronautics. Yet the problem of how to navigate the currents of the air appeared as much a puzzle in 1783 as in the centuries before the balloon was invented.

A century passed before we come to what may be considered the second era in practical aeronautics. The balloon then—thanks to the achievements of such men as Santos-Dumont and Count Ferdinand von Zeppelin—became capable of navigation in the air currents by the use of the internal combustion engine. The dirigible succeeded to the simple gas-balloon. But what was to prove of even greater importance in the history of aviation was the fact that by the end of the nineteenth century men were actively engaged in practical experiments with gliders or planes, built to imitate the wings of birds.

The second era was the period of the invention of the airplane, crowned with the success of Wilbur and Orville Wright. The early years of the twentieth century found the flying plane—the heavier-than-air machine, the counterpart of the wings of a bird—an accomplished fact. The airplane was built; it now remained to see what could be accomplished with it.

We have seen some of the achievements of the third era, the era of aerial flights across continents and oceans. It has been a period of unequalled daring, of adventures worthy of the greatest heroes of history. From Blériot's flight across the English Channel to Lindbergh's flight across the Atlantic Ocean the story runs of marvellous courage, resource, perseverance. Think for a moment what it means to fly into the air supported by what is at best a fragile machine and trust to compass and gasoline-engine to bear one through gales and fog, over mountain peaks and chasms, angry seas and arctic wastes of ice, to the distant goal! There is daring! The men who have accomplished such feats are heroes indeed!

These wonderful aerial adventures have advanced the science of aviation and shown what could be done by airships under various conditions. Blériot flew across the English Channel in a monoplane with a wing spread of about twenty feet and a motor of twenty-five horsepower. His success attracted attention to aviation and now the English Channel is crossed daily by powerful passenger planes. The voyage of the NC4 across the Atlantic Ocean led to the invention of several new instruments of great value in navigation over long distances out of sight of land. The journey of Alcock and Brown showed that the airplane could make its way through fog and rain and steer a straight course in all sorts of winds. When Macready and Kelly made their flight across the continent from New York to California they demonstrated that a plane could be navigated over wide stretches of country by landmarks, highways, railroads, and the lights of cities and villages at night. The round-the-world journey was of great service in supplying information in regard to aviation in a variety of meteorological conditions, in heat and cold, over land and water. Such voyages as that of the English dirigible, the R-34—which flew from England to Long Island and then returned to the British Isles

—and of the dirigible, the ZR-3, afterwards christened the *Los Angeles*—which flew from Friedrichshafen, Germany, to Lakehurst, New Jersey,—established the prowess of that type of airship.

Byrd's flight in the *Josephine Ford* to the North Pole and back and the voyage of the *Norge* from Spitzbergen across the North Pole to Alaska showed that airplane and dirigible are capable of successful navigation in the Arctic regions. Each of these great spectacular flights has added to the knowledge of aviation and has contributed to the invention of improvements in aircraft.

There is another side to the picture. Many balloons —like that double balloon in which Pilâtre des Roziers and a companion attempted to cross from Boulogne to England—crashed to the ground. Some of those who experimented with gliders—like the pioneers Lilienthal and Pilcher—were wrecked when their gliders fell. Many dirigibles and airplanes have dropped from the air and carried many aviators with them.

As we have seen, the competition for the Orteig prize for a flight from New York to Paris, in either direction, had its casualties. Lieutenant-Commander Noel Davis and Lieutenant S. H. Wooster were killed in the wreck of their biplane while making a test flight. Nungesser and Coli took off from France and were lost somewhere on the westward voyage. In attempting the flight from Europe to America other planes with their crews have vanished in the haze of the North Atlantic. The *St. Raphael,* with the Princess Lowenstein-Wertheim, Captain Leslie Hamilton, and Frederick F. Minchin, started from Upavon, England, on August 8, 1927, to fly to Ottawa, Canada, and was lost at sea. The *Endeavour,* with Captain Walter R. G. Hinchliffe and the Hon. Elsie Mackay, set out from Croydon, England, on March 13, 1928, to cross to New York, and disappeared somewhere in the ocean.

On the flight eastward from North America to Europe there have also been casualities. Three planes have been lost: the *Old Glory,* with Lloyd D. Bertaud, John D. Hill, and Philip Payne, which took off from Old Orchard, Maine, to fly to Rome, on September 6, 1927; the airplane of Captain Terry Tully, Lieutenant James Medcalf, and Sir John Carling, who started from Harbor Grace, Newfoundland, to fly to Croydon, England, on September 7, 1927; and the *Dawn,* in which Mrs. Frances Grayson and three companions, setting out from New York on December 23, 1927, were lost somewhere between New York and Harbor Grace, Newfoundland, on the first leg of a flight to Croydon, England.

Mishaps have been frequent in aviation. Yet such have never daunted the spirit of adventurers. Although nothing had been heard of Nungesser and Coli, who had flown from Paris on May 8, 1927, Lindbergh did not hesitate to start out over the ocean in the *Spirit of St. Louis* on May 20, 1927. And after him, during the following month of June, two other

American aviators dared the eastward passage of the North Atlantic.

One of these two was Clarence D. Chamberlin, the other Richard E. Byrd. Chamberlin started from Roosevelt Field, Long Island, on June 4, 1927, in the Bellanca-designed monoplane *Columbia*. As passenger he had Charles A. Levine, a wealthy man much interested in aviation. As Lindbergh had already won the Orteig prize for a flight from New York to Paris Chamberlin proposed to fly the longer distance from New York to Berlin.

The *Columbia* flew a little to the south of the course Lindbergh had taken. Icebergs were seen after leaving Trepassy Bay and fog was encountered. About midnight the aviators saw the lights of a boat and the next day they sighted the steamship *Mauretania,* circled down about her and waved to those aboard. During the afternoon land came into view and at 8.45 P. M. the machine was flying over Cornwall at the southwestern corner of England. Crossing the English Channel, the *Columbia* reached Germany early the next morning. Fog hid the landscape, but presently, descending to get a better view, Chamberlin found that they were above the flying-field at Dormund. The aviators shouted "Berlin?" and the spectators pointed eastward. Now, however, they had used up almost all their gasoline, and therefore, flying a few miles east, they were obliged to land on the outskirts of a small village near Eisleben. They had covered a distance of 3,911 miles in forty-three hours, and had established a new long distance non-stop record.

Byrd set off on his flight across the North Atlantic from Roosevelt Field, Long Island, on June 29, 1927. His machine was the large tri-motored monoplane *America*. The crew was composed of veteran aviators: Byrd, the man who had been the first to fly to the North Pole, Lieutenant George O. Noville, Lieutenant Bernt Balchen, and Bert Acosta.

The *America* rose at 5.24 A. M. Rain was falling, but the Weather Bureau prophesied better conditions over the ocean. When they reached Nova Scotia the sky became clear. The sun was shining as they passed near Halifax, but above Newfoundland they came into thick fog.

In their struggle to get above the fog they used up much gasoline and Byrd presently calculated that if they met with even light winds blowing against them they would alight in the ocean for lack of fuel. His theory was that if they could fly at the proper altitude they would have favoring winds, and on this he staked the success of the voyage. The fog continued, they were flying nearly two miles high, the night air was very cold, and ice formed on the plane. Sometimes they were able to make their way above the clouds, again they had to drive the plane through inky darkness. At 6.50 A. M. on June thirtieth Byrd sent out this radio message: " We have seen neither land nor sea since 3 o'clock yesterday. Everything completely covered with fog. Whatever happens I take my hat off to these great fellows.''

A study of the weather maps led Byrd to conclude that they were being drifted to the south. They picked up a message from a ship and later located the position of the steamship *Paris*. This gave Byrd their own position and he now set his course directly for Finisterre, France.

They had made splendid speed and calculated that the wind had assisted them at a rate of about thirty miles an hour all the way from Newfoundland. Another satisfaction was the discovery that the gasoline gauge was incorrect and that they had, as Noville said, "enough gasoline left to fly to Rome."

In the afternoon of the second day they flew out of the thick clouds and could see the water. Soon they got glimpses of the sun. Now they were picking up many radio messages. Then they sighted land, passed above the seaport of Brest and set their course for Paris.

The weather was clear over that part of France, but it looked thick to the east. Noville radioed to Paris and the word came that there were squalls and fog there. With darkness the *America* ran into storm and rain; again it was a case of flying through inky blackness.

When they thought they should be about above Paris the weather cleared a little and they saw a revolving light that they supposed was the beacon at

Le Bourget field. Looking closer, they discovered to their amazement that the revolving light was flashing above water. It was the beacon of a lighthouse, not that of Le Bourget. There was no such lighthouse near Paris; they must therefore be somewhere on the coast of France!

The compass—inaccurate, as it proved—had led them in a great circle. Checking up their position as well as they could, they set another course for Paris. It was raining very hard on the coast and was even stormier inland. Watching the gasoline gauge, they flew on through the gale, and again arrived where their dead reckoning showed that they should be above Paris. They could see no lights here, however.

In the thick fog and with fuel running low Byrd decided not to try to make a landing in the country, where he might wreck the plane and its crew as well as kill anyone who might be beneath them on the ground. Instead he would turn back to the water and attempt a descent there. With this intention he set a course for the lighthouse they had seen. When he thought they were near it he told Balchen to fly lower. Coming out of the mist, they saw the lighthouse and cruised over it slowly. They could tell they were above the water but could only indistinctly make out the line of the shore. They dropped navigation flares to light up the beach and the ocean; then Byrd gave the word to Balchen to make a landing.

The wheels of the *America* touched the waves, and such was the tremendous resistance of the water that the landing gear and the wheels were ripped from the plane. The *America* immediately filled. Byrd was swimming outside, Noville was climbing out through the window. Byrd swam around to the cockpit, which was under water, and found Balchen freeing himself. Hunting for Acosta, the two dove under the plane. In a moment Acosta appeared and the wrecked aviators climbed on top of a wing.

They were much shaken up, but they managed to pump up the rubber boat they carried in the plane. Shipping the oars, they rowed to shore. Tramping along the beach to the lighthouse they called to the keeper and learned that they were at Ver-sur-Mer, a small town on the coast of France.

Byrd and Balchen later went back to salvage the mail and the records of their journey. The tide had gone out and they found the plane nearly high and dry on the beach. The documents were safe, but the plane itself was a mass of wreckage.

When Byrd and his companions reached Paris they were given a welcome that for enthusiasm almost equalled the one that had been accorded to Lindbergh a month before.

This was a most extraordinary air voyage; the aviators had flown for more than nineteen hours through fog, had reached Paris and then circled away from the city, and had travelled approximately 4,200 miles through the air. For sheer adventure it would be difficult to equal Byrd's flight in the *America* from Long Island to Ver-sur-Mer.

There was one other successful flight in 1927 across the North Atlantic from west to east, in addition to those of Lindbergh, Chamberlin and Byrd. Two American aviators, Edward F. Schlee and William S. Brock, started from Harbor Grace, Newfoundland, on August 27, 1927, in a Stinson monoplane, the *Pride of Detroit,* with the object of attempting to break the record for an air journey around the world. They made a non-stop flight from Harbor Grace to Croydon, England, accomplishing a distance of 2,358 miles in twenty-three hours. From there they flew eastward over Europe and Asia, and reached Tokio on September fourteenth. There, however, they were obliged to give up the attempt to fly across the Pacific Ocean on account of unfavorable weather.

Meanwhile other aviators were daring the Pacific. There had already been much interest in the possibility of flying from California to the Hawaiian Islands. The United States Navy Department had built several seaplanes of a new type, having a flying radius of over 1,900 miles in still air. These seaplanes were known as the PNs. In the spring of 1925 it was decided to attempt the flight from San Francisco to Hawaii with three of these seaplanes.

One of the planes could not be made ready in time for the flight, but on August 31, 1925 two of the seaplanes rose from the water of San Pablo Bay, which forms the northern part of San Francisco Bay. One of these met with mishap and had to be towed back to San Francisco. The other,—designated the PN-9,—in charge of Lieutenant-Commander John Rodgers, flew on out of the Golden Gate and into the haze of the wide Pacific Ocean.

Ships had been stationed to patrol the course, and after three hours of flying the crew of the PN-9 saw through the twilight the first of these vessels. That night the moon was full and the aviators had plenty of light over the ocean. The moon disappeared just before dawn; they ran into a few rain squalls, and with daylight the usual trade-wind commenced to blow. Soon after they picked up the *Langley,* one of the patrol ships.

Presently they checked up the gasoline and found that unless the trade-wind freshened considerably they would be unable to reach Hawaii unless they took on more fuel. Commander Rodgers expected the wind to strengthen about ten o'clock in the morning and his calculation was correct, for the trade-wind began to blow five to six miles an hour. This was not sufficient, however, and Rodgers decided that the wisest course would be to get replenishment from the *Aroostook,* which was the nearest supply ship.

Commander Rodgers says: "I had my chief radioman, O. G. Stantz, get in immediate touch with the *Aroostook.* Stantz told them that we would have to refuel from them, and asked them to please follow us closely with their radio compass so that, in case we should have to make a landing before reaching the ship, they would know our position and could come or send help to us. Other ships in the neighborhood were also advised of our contemplated action."

As the wind did not increase and the supply of gasoline diminished the aviators were more and more in a dilemma. They began to doubt whether they would be able to reach the *Aroostook* before the fuel ran out. Then abruptly both the motors stopped. Instantly Pope, one of the two pilots, motioned to the radio operator to reel in his antenna, which was a long copper wire that trailed some three hundred feet below the plane. Stantz did not obey, and as the PN-9 settled he kept on sending the signal, "Landing, landing, landing," until the antenna hit the water.

They expected to hit the sea pretty hard, but so skillful was the pilot that he brought the plane down from a height of eight hundred feet and lighted on the waves as airily as a gull. The aviators were uninjured and thought themselves fortunate in the fact that the plane had not capsized.

They figured that they were about sixty miles from the *Aroostook,* and that the nearest land would be the island of Kauai, in the Hawaii group. To that goal they now started to sail before the wind. Rodgers says: "Because Stantz had been unable to broadcast our whereabouts when our engine failed, no one but we knew within fifty miles of where we went down, and there was no way of our telling others, as we had no power for sending by our radio."

That night they kept a lookout for vessels and all the next day, but caught no sight of one. In the evening came a message from the *Aroostook*: "PN-9 No. 1, we thought we saw your flare ahead. If you pick this up, please fire star-shell or show light."

Rodgers told Lieutenant Connell to fire the Véry pistol, the best signal light they had. They received no answering signal, however.

Early the following morning the lookout shouted: "Smoke ahead!"

They saw the topmast of a ship just above the horizon, but although they tried to signal to her, after about two hours the vessel disappeared.

They had a supply of provisions, but most of the food had become moldy and was not at all appetizing. "About the only thing that had not molded," says Rodgers, "was our supply of crackers, and these were now all gone. Our canned beef, while free of this defect, was getting strong and unpleasantly salty."

The sea was becoming rougher and rougher, and presently they decided to take off all the fabric from both the lower wings and use it for rigging sails. Then the plane rode more steadily. As day followed day they received reports of planes and ships that were looking for them, but none came into view. There were sharks in the water about them. For several days they encountered rough weather. Lack of fresh food and water made their position more difficult.

Rodgers continues: "Each time we moved about it was done painfully slow. Each time we changed the rigging of our sails, it required a forced effort. We were so weak that we ran a line from the bow to the stern, so that we could grab the line in case of a sudden lurch of the craft, and thus save ourselves from providing a meal for our hangers-on, the tiger-sharks.

"I had kept out two canteens of water, and issued this very sparingly and impartially to the boys, a half-cupful at a time. Monday this water was all gone. It was a question then just how much longer we could last without another swallow.

"I knew that we had sailed about three hundred miles by this time, averaging about fifty miles a day. Examining the chart, I made out our position to be near Oahu. This calculation was confirmed when, on Tuesday night, we saw the Army searchlights located at Schofield Barracks, Oahu. This was the first sign of life we had seen after the strange steamer passed us on the preceeding Thursday."

They sighted the island of Oahu, but when they worked out their position they decided to change their course and try to sail to Kauai, which, although farther away, gave promise of providing a better port. As they sailed on this new tack, they ran into rain, for which they were very grateful, as it enabled them to obtain fresh drinking water by catching the down-pour in the hollows of the sails and in thermos bottles and canteens. Thursday morning the weather cleared and they saw the outlines of Kauai. By afternoon they were within ten miles of the island. Then they discovered that they were likely to run onto a rocky shore after nightfall. To swim through that surf would be almost impossible for them. They sent up smoke signals of distress and after about fifteen minutes one of the crew yelled: "There's a submarine aft of us!"

The submarine came within hailing distance and the aviators called over for food and water. The rescuing craft threw them a heaving-line and then put aboard the plane five gallons of water and a quantity of fresh provisions. Then they were towed into port and rowed ashore, to be welcomed by all the inhabitants of the village of Lihue.

The PN-9 had reached Hawaii from San Francisco after a flight of 1,870 miles, followed by a sail of 450 miles. That voyage over the sea had been a remarkable record of endurance.

In the summer of the year that saw the flights of Lindbergh, Chamberlin and Byrd across the Atlantic the first successful non-stop flight from California to Hawaii was made by two United States Army aviators, Lieutenants Lester J. Maitland and Albert F. Hegenberger. These two started from Oakland, California, on June 28, 1927, in a large trimotored Fokker monoplane and after flying for twenty-five hours and fifty minutes landed safely at Honolulu. This flight, which covered 2,400 miles, was the longest yet made entirely across water.

The South Atlantic Ocean, as has already been related, was flown across by Major Franco of Spain and his companions in the flying-boat *Ne Plus Ultra* in

January, 1926. This voyage was made, however, with stops at the Canary, the Cape Verde, and the Fernando Noronha Islands. Other aviators succeeded in crossing the South Atlantic from the Old World to the New by breaking their flights at different islands on the coast of Africa and South America. Then, on October 15, 1927, two Frenchmen, Dieudonne Costes and Joseph Le Brix, set out from St. Louis, Senegal, Africa, and made a non-stop flight of 2,000 miles to Pernambuco, Brazil. The elapsed time for their journey was twenty-one hours and fifteen minutes.

Another remarkable air voyage in which the Atlantic Ocean was crossed twice was that of the Italian aviator Commander Francesco di Pinedo and his companions in a large-sized Savoia flying-boat. This journey was described as a "Four Continent Tour." Starting from Rome on February 13, 1927, Pinedo crossed from the Cape Verde Islands to Brazil. He then flew north over South and Central America and the United States and in June took off from Newfoundland, aiming to reach the Azores. The flying-boat was forced to descend a short distance from the islands, but after floating on the sea for two days was towed to port. Pinedo then resumed his journey and flew on to Rome, where he landed on June sixteenth, having covered a distance of 30,000 miles.

To carry a message of good-will to the people of Mexico and Central and South America was the purpose of a flight on which Colonel Charles A. Lindbergh set out on December 13, 1927. He flew alone and accomplished the voyage of 2,200 miles to Mexico City in twenty-seven hours and ten minutes. At the Valbuena field he was welcomed by a crowd of 150,-000 Mexicans, and President Calles proclaimed a national holiday in Lindbergh's honor. From Mexico City he flew to Guatemala City, to Belize in Honduras, and to San Salvador, which he reached on January first. All along his route he was received with great demonstrations of welcome. From San Salvador he went on by this itinerary: Tegucigalpa, Honduras; Managua, Nicaragua; San José, Costa Rica; Panama; Colon; Cartagena, Colombia; Bogota, Colombia; Caracas, Venezuela; St. Thomas, Virgin Islands; San Juan, Porto Rico; Santo Domingo; Port au Prince, Haiti; Havana, Cuba; and St. Louis, Missouri. He arrived at St. Louis on February 13, 1928. He had flown 9,390 miles and his "good-will flight" had been an immense success.

In furtherance of this same idea of cultivating good fellowship among peoples the dirigible *Los Angeles* made a journey from the United States to Panama.

The North Atlantic had not yet been crossed from Europe to North America, and to achieve this difficult enterprise—considered much more hazardous than the flight from west to east because of wind conditions—was the object of three daring aviators, Baron Gunther von Huenefeld and Captain Hermann Koehl, both Germans, and Commandant James Fitzmaurice, an Irishman, who hoped to fly from

Ireland to Mitchel Field, New York. They started in the Junkers monoplane *Bremen* early in the morning of April 12, 1928, from Baldonnel Field, Dublin, Ireland. For hours they battled with storms but managed to wing their way westward. Headwinds drove them out of their course and ultimately, after flying for thirty-four hours, they were obliged to land on Greenely Island in Belle Isle Straits, a small island that lies between the southeastern tip of Labrador and the northwestern shore of Newfoundland. They had crossed the North Atlantic, however, and the *Bremen* had made the first non-stop flight from Ireland to North America. Great was the reception given the three aviators for their memorable achievement.

The excitement caused by the voyage of the *Bremen* was at its height when news came of another remarkable aerial journey. Two aviators had flown over "the roof of the world," and had from the air surveyed previously unexplored regions of the North Polar tract. The two were Captain George H. Wilkins, an Australian, and Lieutenant Carl Ben Eielson, a Norwegian. Starting from Point Barrow, Alaska, in a Lockheed-Vega monoplane on April 15, 1928, they flew for twenty hours over the wide wastes of the Polar seas. The route they took was about two hundred miles south of the North Pole and across the barren Arctic regions of water and floating ice that lie between the Pole and the top of the American continent.

Fighting through all sorts of winds, Wilkins and

Eielson were at length compelled by a blizzard to bring their plane down on the island of Dead Man's Point, which is located on the northern side of Isfjord and is about thirty miles north of Green Harbor, a small coal mining town of Spitzbergen.

On this desolate and uninhabited island the aviators were held weather-bound for five days. Then they were able to resume their journey and continued on in the monoplane to Svalbard, Spitzbergen. That place they reached on April twenty-first, after an actual air journey from Point Barrow, Alaska, of twenty and one-half hours.

The voyage of the *Bremen* and the Wilkins expedition were both wonderful achievements in the story of aviation.

II

While aviators have been adventuring over seas, ice-fields and deserts the commercial or business side of aviation has made most interesting developments. Airships are being used for the transportation of mail, freight and passengers and what are called airways are acquiring importance.

An airway has no metal tracks like a railroad. It is essentially a route through the air, but it also includes the airdromes at the ends of the route, the intermediate landing stations, and the organization, both of men and apparatus, that facilitates aerial

The Monoplane *Columbia* Reaches Germany

Costes and LeBrix Flying Around the Atlantic

travel. In Europe many important airways have been established. Croydon, outside London, is the headquarters of the Imperial Airways, Ltd. In addition to the regular English aerial service the Croydon airdrome is used by a number of foreign companies as their London terminal. These companies are the French Air Union; the Deutsche Luft Hansa, a German organization; the Royal Dutch Air Line, popularly designated the K. L. M.; and the Brussels Company, the Société Anonyme Belge d'Exploitation de la Navigation Aérienne. From Croydon one may travel by air to many European cities; the English company, Imperial Airways, Ltd., runs services to Paris, Brussels, Amsterdam, Cologne, Basle, and Zurich.

Airways in other parts of Europe have also been developed. One may fly from Zurich by way of Munich, Vienna, Budapest, and Belgrade to Bukharest; or from Vienna to Prague, Breslau, Warsaw, and Danzig. From Berlin there is an aerial service to Copenhagen, and from there to Malmö, in Sweden. From Malmö there is a route to Hamburg and Amsterdam, and so back to London.

In the south of France an airway offers service from Toulouse to Perpignan, and thence to Barcelona and across the Mediterranean Sea to Alicante. Airways radiate from Alicante to Algiers, Oran, and Malaga. From Perpignan there is an airway to Marseilles; from Nice to Ajaccio, in Corsica; and from Rabat to Oran. Thus a wonderful network of aerial travel is being worked out over Europe and its environs.

The Croydon field is a busy scene. One may see a Handley-Page plane setting out for Paris, an Armstrong "Argosy" getting off for Cologne, a Fokker monoplane of the Royal Dutch Air Line leaving for Rotterdam and Amsterdam, a "Goliath" of the French Air Union starting for Le Bourget, on the outskirts of Paris.

In many ways the aerial service offers the most convenient method of travel. Take the journey from London to Paris, for example. To accomplish it by land and sea requires seven hours or more; one travels to the English coast by train, embarks in a steamer for the trip across the Channel, and then takes another train for the journey to Paris. By the air liner one arrives at Le Bourget in less than three hours after leaving Croydon. No changes are needed, and the airplane provides a maximum of comfort. The cabin of the air liner is entirely enclosed, though the windows on each side may be opened if desired; there are two rows of seats, one on each side of a central aisle, and above the seats are racks for luggage. The pilots are experienced aviators, accustomed to flying in all kinds of weather.

To guide the pilots through fog various safeguards are employed. There are guiding lamps on the ground as well as on the tops of tall buildings along the airway. These lamps are filled with "neon" gas, which gives a red light with remarkable fog-piercing properties. Near the Croydon field there is one of these "neon" beacons that is visible at a distance of fifty miles.

These beacons are of great value to the pilot in travel at night as well as in mist and fog, and on the London-Paris airway they have been located at Tatsfield, Penshurst, Cranbrook, Lympne, Littlestone, and St. Inglevert in addition to those at Croydon and Le Bourget. A great aerial lighthouse has also been built on top of Mont Afrique, near Dijon, France; this has a beam of 1,000,000,000 candlepower and is visible in clear weather for 300 miles.

The London-Paris commercial air service was started in August, 1919, and in the following six years British commercial planes flew approximately 5,000,000 miles between London and the continent, and carried more than 60,000 passengers and many hundreds of tons of freight.

Western Australia has been one of the chief countries to benefit from the use of airways. In that territory there is a population of about 300,000 people scattered over an area of some 1,000,000 square miles. The larger part of the inhabitants are settled in towns along the coast, Perth, Geraldton, Carnarvon, each town situated at a great distance from its neighbors. North of Geraldton communication was until recently entirely by steamer and there were frequently intervals of several weeks between steamer calls. The lack of good roads was also a great handicap to those who lived inland.

A company with the title of Western Australian Airways, Ltd., was organized in August, 1921, to furnish airplane service from Perth in the south to Derby in the north, with stations at Geraldton, Carnarvon, and many other places. This company has a government contract to carry mail. It has shortened the journey from Perth to Derby from seven days to fifty-six hours, and brought the widely-separated towns of Western Australia into easy reach of each other as well as expediting transportation of passengers and freight to and from other parts of the continent.

In the United States airways have been developed largely for use in the carriage of mail. The first experimental line was inaugurated by the Post Office Department in 1918, connecting New York and Washington, but this was discontinued after a few months. In 1919 the Post Office Department began an air mail service across the continent, but this was not a "through" service, as the planes only carried the mail in daylight and handed it over to the railroads for carriage at night. The first of these Post Office planes were used between Cleveland and Chicago on May 15, 1919, and afterwards the air route was extended from Cleveland to New York. In May, 1920 the air service stretched west from Chicago to Omaha, and in September, 1920, air mail planes were flying between Omaha and San Francisco. This completed what might be called a combination daylight-airplane and night-railroad service across the United

States. The mail was carried by plane from New York in the morning and was put on a train in Chicago in the evening; the following morning another plane took it and flew with it over the rest of the route.

To make night flying safe guiding lights were needed and the Post Office Department experimented with various types of powerful beacons and illuminated landing fields. Then the government established at Chicago, Iowa City, Omaha, North Platte, and Cheyenne very powerful revolving searchlights that sent out beams of 450,000,000 candlepower. These lights have been sighted at a distance of over 130 miles and can be ordinarily seen for 100 miles. As the beacons are placed only about 200 miles apart, the pilot is able in clear weather to sight the one ahead before he is out of sight of the one astern.

To mark the route in misty weather additional beacons of 4,000,000 candlepower are situated at intervals of 25 to 30 miles between the main searchlights, and between these secondary beacons others of 5,000 candlepower are stationed at every third mile. The main landing grounds are near the main searchlights and the emergency fields close to the secondary lights. In addition each machine has powerful searchlights attached to its wings to help the pilot in finding his way.

This system of illumination has enabled the government to send air mail planes by night as well as by day. In July, 1924 a "through" air service was established; the stations at which the planes descended to transfer their freight or take on fresh pilots were, including the two terminal points; New York, Bellefonte, Cleveland, Bryan, Chicago, Iowa City, Rock Springs, Salt Lake City, Elko, Reno, and San Francisco.

The ordinary schedule time for the journey from coast to coast was 33 hours. The ordinary mail train took from 96 to 120 hours. It is interesting to note that in 1860 the carriage of a letter from New York to San Francisco by train and pony express involved a journey of 10½ days. Business has therefore benefited tremendously by the United States Post Office air mail service.

This service is carried on more or less regardless of weather conditions. Many of the pilots have had strange adventures. One of them while crossing high mountains near Salt Lake City ran into a terrific blizzard, and his plane was hurled against a mountain side with such force that the landing-carriage was smashed. The pilot was stranded in deep snow on a peak 9,400 feet above sea level. Fastening his travelling bag to his shoulders, he started down the mountain, setting his course by compass. He had to wade waist-deep through snow, but he fought his way through it all that day and the next night. At daylight he reached the timber line. By then he was almost exhausted by his efforts and the biting cold, but fortunately he sighted a barn and after pushing on for a mile came to a house. Two days later he was able to ride to the nearest post-office and telephone to Salt Lake City, and from the government office there he learned that for several days all the planes of that division of the Air Mail Service had been hunting for him.

Another pilot struck a mountain at a height of 8,200 feet and as his plane tore through the trees it was completely wrecked by the branches. The aviator was thrown out and his left shoulder was dislocated. As he descended the mountain he fell heavily and the fall, by great good luck, actually replaced his dislocated shoulder. He made his way to some railroad tracks, held up the next train, and rode aboard it to the neighboring station.

The Post Office Department has developed a contract system of feeders to the transcontinental line and as a result the air mail service has branched in many directions. There are lines between most of the important cities. These lines carry mail and some of them also carry passengers and freight. When the transcontinental airway showed promise of being a financial success the government turned it over to a private company. The Seattle-Victoria, Pilottown-New Orleans, and Key West-Havana lines are run in connection with foreign air mail services.

Improvements are constantly being made in the construction of the various types of monoplanes and biplanes, in the engines, in the devices that make for more skillful management, in the safeguards of the aviators. Different countries have built different patterns and the widely diverse uses to which the planes are put call for a great range of designs of construction. This is equally so of the seaplanes and flying-boats that are built to rise from and land upon the water. The difference between the seaplane and the flying-boat is in the form of the landing-gear. In the seaplane, hydroplane floats are substituted for the wheeled landing chassis and in some models the construction of airplane and seaplane is interchangeable, so that the machine may be converted from one type to the other simply by removing the pneumatic-tired wheels and replacing them by floats, a tail float taking the place of the ordinary tail skid, and additional floats being placed under the tips of the lower wings to keep them out of the water.

In the flying-boat, the boat hull takes the place of the regular fuselage or body construction, so that the pilot and crew are accommodated well below the level of the lower wings instead of being seated above them as in the usual type of airplane or seaplane. Neither the seaplane nor the flying-boat is as speedy a machine as those of similar wing and motor power built for use over the land; the floats or boat hull present a much greater resistance to the wind; on the other hand, the pilots of the seaplanes and flying-boats have the great advantage of being able to land anywhere in the water in case of need.

The parachute is the lifebelt of the air. It was used early in the history of ballooning and the credit for the first really successful parachute descent belongs to a Frenchman, André Jacques Garnerin. Garnerin ascended on October 22, 1797 from the park of Monceau, Paris, on a parachute that was attached to a balloon, and when he was at a height of 2,000 feet he cut the connecting rope. The balloon rose and burst; the parachute descended, swinging from side to side; Garnerin landed safely and, mounting a horse, rode back triumphantly to the starting place, where he was received with cheers by the admiring crowd. In 1802 he made the first parachute descent ever seen in England and afterwards many times demonstrated the safety of the invention.

Many aviators have saved themselves from being dashed to the ground by the use of a parachute. Lieutenant John A. Macready, who with a companion made the first non-stop flight across North America, was flying by night from Columbus to Dayton, Ohio, on June 19, 1914. His engine stopped while he was about 3,000 feet above the ground. To descend in the darkness on rough country might well be disastrous. Macready says:

"I loosened my safety belt and threw one leg over the side of the ship, keeping one hand on the control stick. Finally I crawled out on the wing and attempted to nose the ship up, so that I could leave without danger of having the parachute catch.

"I let go of the plane and let the wind blow me free. I decided to count two before I pulled the ripcord of the parachute, so as not to foul the plane. I don't know in what position I was when I left the ship, whether I was upside down or not. But I heard the parachute open with a snap and I knew I would land safely in some place.''

He landed on the edge of a cliff. The plane had crashed to the ground and was on fire. Great was the relief and amazement of the crowd when the aviator appeared among them entirely unhurt.

A new chapter in the history of airships was inaugurated by the first flight of an airplane from a passenger steamship to land. Clarence D. Chamberlin, the hero of the first flight from New York to Germany, ascended on August 1, 1927 in a Fokker biplane from the deck of the *Leviathan* when that steamship was eighty-two miles out at sea. He encountered storm and fog, but landed one hour and twenty-five minutes later at Curtiss Field, Long Island. Chamberlain's biplane rose from the steamship's deck by its own power; the United States Navy Department plans to shoot or catapult planes from the decks of ships by means of a 50-foot runway, which will enable the machines to attain a speed of 50-miles-an-hour in that distance.

The United States Navy Department has several airplane carriers, the *Langley,* which was a pioneer in this type of ship, and the *Saratoga* and the *Lexington,* the most modern developments in this new field. The *Saratoga* and the *Lexington* are in most respects sister ships and are altogether unique vessels. The *Saratoga* has a two-acre landing deck, a secret catapult and a secret arresting gear that is designed to bring a plane to a stop on the landing deck within four times the length of the plane. This ship is able to carry eighty-three pursuit, reconnaissance and bombing planes in its storage quarters and on the hangar deck, and the planes are raised or lowered to and from the landing deck by electric elevators. She is not built upward with lofty masts and gun turrets like a dreadnaught, but she has a considerable armament and is capable of making a greater speed than any other ship afloat.

The ship presents a flat and very massive appearance; the landing deck extends 885 feet over all in length, 106 feet in breadth, and 74 feet from keel to landing stage. There are two main decks, the landing stage above and the hangar deck below, and the four electric elevators that work between the two decks have been so constructed that their tops are flush with the upper deck, since nothing must break the smooth surface that is used for take-offs and landings. Planes can rise from the deck or alight on it in almost any weather, and when conditions are favorable seaplanes may be lowered over the ship's side by a crane, located forward of a gun turret. The *Saratoga* also carries aboard fully-equipped foundries, machine and repair shops, and a woodworking plant, everything needed to build or repair airplanes and seaplanes.

In addition to its use of airplane carriers the Navy

Department purposes to catapult planes from battle-ships. The propulsive power of these catapults is either gunpowder or compressed air and the planes used are seaplanes. If ocean liners make use of the catapulting system it should prove very valuable in expediting the transfer of mail from ship to shore.

Airplanes have shown their worth in a multitude of ways and new uses for aircraft are continually appearing. A fleet of ships some years ago were frozen up in the Gulf of Finland, far from shore. The crews would have been in a perilous position had not a plane dropped provisions and supplies on their decks. Fishing boats were lost off the western coast of Ireland; airplanes hunted above the islands for the vessels and furnished food to the famished fishermen. In North America flying machines patrol great areas on the watch for forest fires and signal or carry word of any signs of flames to the fire-fighting stations. In one season such an aerial patrol discovered more than six hundred fires and by giving warning was able to save timber that was worth many millions of dollars.

Another important use of the airplane is in the spraying of crops with chemicals designed to stop the inroads of harmful insects. The plane can scatter the chemicals far and wide and has proved the farmer's greatest aid in protecting his fields from invasion. It is also able to sow seeds more quickly than any other machine; in twenty minutes an airplane has sown an

entire square mile of ground with grass seed and accomplished what would have needed the labor of a
couple of men for two or three weeks.

The airplane is also of great service to engineers in
making preliminary surveys for roads or railroads
since the aviator can photograph great areas much
more expeditiously than a surveyor could traverse
them on foot. This work is specially valuable in
charting swampy country or thickly wooded territory. The Royal Canadian Air Force has been of
great use to the government in making maps of sections not yet developed and in 1925 this Air Force
photographed 47,700 square miles.

The United States Coast Guard has its seaplanes
and flying-boats used for many purposes: to carry aid
to persons or ships in peril along the shore, to patrol
the waters for derelicts, to locate schools of fish for
fishermen, to search for icebergs and inform vessels
of the position of these floating frozen mountains,
and to provide assistance to lighthouse keepers on iso-
lated rocks.

How valuable is the airplane in derelict hunting
may be shown from the fact that in 1927 the scouting
service of the Coast Guard planes led to the removal
of 101 of these maritime perils. An odd assortment
they were; the derelicts included rafts, logs, scows,
mines, spars, skiffs, canoes, motor-boats, buoys,
schooners, barges, docks, trees, wooden cribs and duck
blinds.

III

Aviation presents innumerable interesting fields of study and of exploration and the uses of the airship are being developed in a wide variety of different directions. Let us take two examples from among many. The experimental flight of the new United States Navy seaplane PN-12 is reported to have added approximately 28 per cent to the cruising range of the seaplane. On one sustained flight the PN-12 covered a distance greater than that between the important landfalls on the transoceanic routes of the world and remained in the air longer that did Lindbergh's plane on his famous flight from New York to Paris. The PN-12 is a much slower machine than a plane such as Lindbergh's, because of the heavy body weight it carries, but it can alight easily on the water, make repairs, and take off again from a rough sea. Aviation experts look to the seaplane as the best vehicle for transoceanic air traffic in heavier-than-air craft.

Another interesting development is the exploration of the Arctic regions by airplanes. Captain George H. Wilkins has shown what may be done in that field and General Umberto Nobile has been engaged on aerial voyages of study and experimentation in the area north of Spitzbergen. These flights are of particular value in establishing the long-projected scheme of a safe intercontinental airway over the

Arctic ice fields. Such a route might prove of the greatest importance in commercial traffic between widely separated lands.

When we consider the possibilities of such flights as these and realize what has already been done by aviators in the Arctic area we appreciate that the air has indeed become a marvellous medium of travel. Rash would it be to prophesy concerning this new method of transportation and communication. Yet the opinions of expert students of aviation are interesting; for instance, their views on the possibility of a regular passenger and mail service across the ocean by airplane. Many of them argue against it and for the reason that a high rate of speed is impossible in a machine built to carry passengers and freight.

One plane may have great speed, another a long cruising range, a third great carrying capacity, and a fourth the ability to make a slow landing and a quick take-off; but all of these qualities have not been combined as yet in any one plane. Airplane builders have learned that as a general principle one horsepower of motive force will support and drive at a fairly high speed a total weight of about twenty-five pounds. This total weight includes the weight of the machine, engine, propeller, fuel, passengers, freight. Where the ratio of total weight is greater in relation to the horsepower there is a resulting loss in speed, in ability to control the plane, and in safety. Therefore where the weight of the motive force, the engine, gasoline and oil, is increased in order to secure greater power the amount of that increased weight must be subtracted from the weight of the rest of the plane, fuselage, wings, passengers, and freight, so as to keep the proper ratio of one horsepower to every twenty-five pounds. The remarkable success of recent flights has been due, it has been pointed out, to the reduction in the weight of the engines.

The builders of planes are not so much interested in constructing larger planes as they are in making the machines more reliable in manipulation and safer in flight. Their object is to make them of greater commercial use and therefore to decrease the cost of construction and the consumption of gasoline and oil. This will add to the popular use of the airplane, but for short-range journeys rather than for such long distances as transoceanic flights.

The long air voyages will be undertaken, in the view of many students of aviation, by such men as Lindbergh, Chamberlin, Byrd, Wilkins, and others, who wish to achieve unusual results, to explore new territories or obtain new scientific data, and will not probably lead to an organized passenger and mail service across the Atlantic or Pacific Oceans. This for the reason that planes built to carry passengers and freight such distances at a high rate of speed would be too heavy for the motive power required to drive them. In other words, the weight of the engine and the weight of the plane cannot both be increased; to do so would be to imperil the all-important factor of safety.

For long distance commercial voyages the dirigible airship possesses many advantages over the airplane.

For other commercial purposes, however, the plane is proving of great value. In Europe, as we have seen, airplanes carry a great many passengers and a great amount of freight in all directions. In the United States the passenger service is at present negligible, but the air mail is rapidly developing, new routes are being mapped out, and the airways will soon reach to all sections of the country. There is no reason to believe that when the American public becomes used to aerial travel there will be less passenger service in the United States than there is already in Europe.

The airplane for practical purposes must be able to take on fresh supplies of fuel at regular intervals and to chart its course with reliability; these can be done on land, where there are well lighted airways, frequent landing fields, and fully equipped service stations. On the ocean there are none of these aids; the airplane has to battle through storm and fog and if it is compelled to descend to the water it may be at some place hundreds of miles from a shore or ship.

The land service is an essential factor of safety in the use of the airplane. Possibly some time in the future there will be reliable airways across the ocean, great landing-stages moored to the bed of the sea on which planes may land, refuel or make repairs, and from which they may take off again; but such projects seem visionary now; the expense and difficulty of establishing such islands where the depth of the ocean is very great appear prohibitive. Again, however, it is hazardous to prophesy. The ocean may some day have its dependable airways.

Airplane engines are constantly being improved, and as the stalling of the engine over the land at night or over the ocean at any time is one of the chief reasons for accidents, the greater reliability of the engine will greatly increase the safety of the plane. The increased use of the radio should also be a great aid to the success of air travel. Radio stations will send a continual stream of messages to the winging plane and radio information from shore and ships may take the place of beacons to guide the aviator above the sea. The compass will not be so important; the pilot will set his course by radio directions.

The official weather maps of government Weather Bureaus are a great aid to aviators, especially in reporting areas of fog and storm over the ocean, and as this coastwise service is improved aircraft pilots will be better able to choose the most favorable atmospheric conditions for over-sea flights.

The aviator has instruments in his plane to tell him the altitude of the machine, the approximate speed it is making, and in clear weather how much it is drifting. A most important invention would be an instrument to indicate the drift of the plane when it is flying through fog or above the clouds. With such a device and with improvements in the other instruments of navigation the pilot of a plane should be able to check his position with almost as much reliability as does the pilot of a modern steamship.

The ability to fly through the air is a wonderful achievement, one of the great steps in the story of transportation, that began with the first rude cart on wheels and the first raft that floated on the water. The wheeled vehicle became a carriage, a coach; the raft became a boat, a ship, propelled by oars and sails. Then the steam-engine was invented, and Robert Fulton and others turned the boat into a steamship while George Stephenson took the coach, set it upon rails, fastened it to a steam-driven locomotive, and made the first steam-railroad. Others applied the new motive power to horseless carriages and so produced the automobile. Transportation by land and sea, through the agency of the steam-engine, was the achievement of the nineteenth century.

Travel by air, by the dirigible airship or the airplane, is the accomplishment of the twentieth century. Aircraft assumes in the air the important place that is held by the steamship and the motor-boat on the water, the railroad and the automobile on the land. Its uses are as various as theirs; as it is yet in its infancy one cannot tell what influence it will have on the world's affairs.

When we consider the enthusiasm with which the heroes of aviation have been received in the lands to which they have flown we feel justification for the hope that the airship may bring the peoples of the world to a better understanding of each other and so knit them in the bonds of brotherhood. The airship may become an all-important instrument of good will, as the *Spirit of St. Louis* has been. It may draw races closer together in amity and friendship and so help to further lasting peace among nations. Greater than any other achievement, immeasurably greater than its value in commerce or exploration, will be the high destiny of the airship if it succeeds in spreading knowledge, friendship, and enduring peace.

CHAPTER XXII

THE RECENT ADVENTURERS

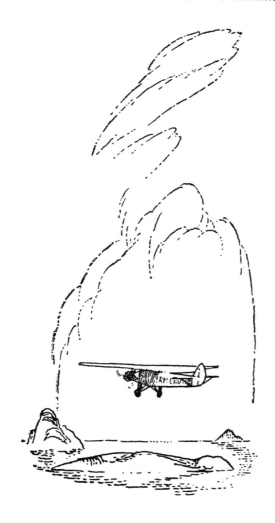

XXII

THE RECENT ADVENTURERS

I

TWO flights of importance occurred in the months of May and June, 1928. The first and most remarkable was the flight of the tri-motor Fokker monoplane *Southern Cross* from San Francisco to Australia. The ship was manned by two Australians, Captain Charles Kingsford-Smith and Charles Ulm, who were the pilots; and two Americans, Harry W. Lyon, navigator, and James Warner, radio operator.

Preparations for this flight had been made with the utmost care, and its successful completion was due as much to the intelligent preparation as to the courage of the crew. During much of their flying they were guided by radio, probably depending more upon this than any aviators on any previous flight. Although they battled with storm during most of the long over-water hops there was never any emergency to which the plane and the crew were not equal.

The *Southern Cross* took off from Oakland, California, on Thursday, May 31. They were in communication with radio stations on land or with ships at sea for almost the entire 2400 miles. The passage was only moderately stormy and with the exception of one moment toward the end when there seemed to be some doubt as to their position there were no unforeseen incidents. They landed at 6 P.M. on Saturday and after a day's rest started the longest hop, from Honolulu to the island of Suva, one of the Fiji Island group in the South Pacific. On this solitary island in the tropics, a low-lying coral island with a few black and torn volcanic peaks, the British Colonial Government had turned Albert Park into an aviation field, giving the flyers sufficient area for landing.

The distance from Barking Sands, where the *Southern Cross* took off from the island Kauai, to Suva, is 3138 miles. No plane had ever flown this distance over water. The first half of the journey to the equator was accomplished without undue trouble. The three motors, running smoothly, maintained a ninety-mile speed. The two Australian pilots alternating at the controls kept the ship at an altitude of about six-hundred feet, where they secured the greatest mileage from their gasoline. Through the clear weather they sailed above smooth seas, with only an occasional light tropic rainstorm to bother them, and luncheon to interrupt the monotonous passage. By radio they communicated to Honolulu Naval Station telling of the smooth journey with "all the comforts of home," but with night-

The *Southern Cross* Flying from San Francisco
to Australia

The *Friendship* Carrying the First Woman Across
the Atlantic

fall conditions changed. They encountered head winds and the violent rainstorms of the South Pacific.

They were obliged to alter their course continually to avoid the heavier storms, and at times to seek an altitude above eight thousand feet. The constellation from which the ship took its name was obscured by clouds and the radio reports told of bumpy air, bad currents, and several falls, through air-pockets, of four hundred feet or more.

The rough weather lowered their gasoline supply to the danger point and the messages reaching an anxious world, while still cheerful and courageous, gave hint of the desperate battle they were having. Daylight brought better weather, and at the end of thirty-four hours and thirty-three minutes they landed on the tiny field at Suva. In two hops they had covered 5538 miles, of the total 7800.

The resolution of the pilots and the skill of their navigator had brought them successfully across the lonely waste of the Pacific, setting a record for flight above water.

The radio log of the *Southern Cross* will remain a record of high courage maintained in dangerous situations, and of a sense of humor never lost. When nearing Fanning Island, twelve miles south of the Hawaiian group, Warner, the radio man, called the station with; "Hello, old man. Nice place. Hope we have permission to trespass upon your domain."

No time was lost at Suva. The plane was overhauled, refueled, and after a brief rest they took off to fly the 1762 miles to Brisbane, Australia. Although this was the shortest distance they had to cover it turned out to be the most dangerous. Throughout the journey the plane fought head winds and storms. They reached Brisbane at ten o'clock on June 9, to receive the applause of the city and the congratulations of the entire world. From Brisbane they went on five hundred miles to Sidney, where the great flight ended.

II

While these four men were making aviation history, two men and a girl, with no fanfare of publicity and with only a half-dozen spectators, left Boston harbour in another three-motored Fokker monoplane and flew from there on the first lap of what was to be a flight to London. Amelia Earhart, social worker in Boston, herself a qualified pilot with five hundred solo hours to her credit; Wilmer Stultz, one of America's leading pilots; and Louis Gordon, co-pilot, were the crew. The plane had originally been built for Commander Byrd to use in his projected flight to the South Pole.

This attempt had been as carefully planned as the Australian expedition. The pilots had received from Commander Byrd all the information that he had gathered during his flight the previous year. The plane was equipped with pontoons in case of a forced landing at sea, and no effort had been spared to make the flight ultimately successful. The hop to Trepassey, Newfoundland, was accomplished without trouble but there bad weather held them for ten days. On the 17th of June, in spite of the adverse weather reports, the monoplane rose easily and headed into the fogs of the Grand Banks. Various messages were received reporting the position of the plane, and twenty-two hours after the take-off the *Friendship* was sighted at Burryport in South Wales. After circling over the town they made a perfect landing on the river. While the presence of Miss Earhart as a member of the crew gave the flight a romantic aura, from the standpoint of aviation it was in all respects a triumph. The entire two thousand miles had to be flown by the aid of instruments, as at no time were the pilots able to secure the position by a sight of either the sun or stars. Constant fog and intermittent rain obscured the entire route. It was not until they were within seventy miles of the British Isles that they were able to see below them the water of the Atlantic.

In piloting his ship "blind" across the ocean Wilmer Stultz proved himself to be among the greatest aviators in the world. They reached the coast of Wales within a mile of where they had calculated to arrive, and only the gasoline supply being low and bad weather indicated, prevented them from flying across and landing at Southampton, their original destination.

The use of three-motored planes in long distance
flying as advocated by Commander Byrd and other
leading figures in aviation, was proven on both these
adventures, and the jinx which had pursued planes
carrying women was finally settled. The following
day the flyers continued on to Southampton where
they were enthusiastically received. Both of these
flights did a great deal to advance long distance flying. They demonstrated that a plane with reserve
power driven by three motors and piloted by men
who are trained navigators need not fear fog or any
normal storm conditions.

Beginning in advance of these two adventures,
continuing while they were in progress, and extend-
ing beyond them, one of the most tragic and dramatic happenings in the history of aviation was taking
place among the bitter, unknown regions beyond
Spitzbergen, involving General Umberto Nobile,
who had the previous year with Lincoln Ellsworth
and Roald Amundsen, flown the airship *Norge* across
the North Pole. During the winter a new dirigible,
the *Italia,* had been built for further exploration in
the north. Nobile was put in command of this expedition which flew from Italy by easy stages to
Kings Bay, Spitzbergen. There in the early part of
May two expeditions were made in an attempt to
seek the chimerical Crocker Land. The first flight
was not notable, and the second lasted more than
seventy hours, during which time the *Italia* covered
a distance of 2375 miles. No new land was discovered,

but much uncharted land was mapped and photographed. The second flight was made under adverse weather conditions, the cold being so intense that the drinking water, tea, coffee, meat and bread were frozen.

After a brief rest the *Italia* put out again to fly across the Pole and continue the investigations. For the first part of the trip everything went well. The dirigible reached the Pole and started on the return. Immediately violent storms were encountered and the ship blown far from its course. Radio communication was maintained for some time, and finally that ceased. Almost a week of silence followed. Then out of the air came the S O S signal and the story of danger and disaster. Becoming unmanageable the *Italia* had plunged to the ice about twenty miles north of Cape Leigh Smith on the eastern extremity of the North East Land and approximately 220 miles from the base ship *Citta di Milano*, anchored in Kings Bay. The radio messages were quite faint and not explicit. No one knew exactly what had happened, except that the plight of the lost crew was desperate and all the resources of Italy, Sweden, and of individual men, were called upon for the rescue. The messages continued to arrive and gradually the entire story was revealed to an anxious world. In the plunge of the dirigible onto the ice pack nine men of the crew had been thrown, and the forward gondola wrecked, scattering provisions and instruments, including the radio apparatus, upon the ice. The dirigible then rose again and disappeared from view, drifting eastward and carrying with it the seven remaining members of the crew. Both General Nobile and the Chief Engineer were badly injured in the crash, and the men were without medicine or means of protection. Later, the Engineer died of his injuries.

Having located the lost explorers expeditions were started by dog team, on ice breakers, and by air, to their relief. All nations came to their help. From Russia the most powerful ice breakers started, Norwegian and Swedish flyers with seaplanes were commissioned to fly over the desolate waste in an attempt to locate the camp of General Nobile and his men, and crack dog teams started overland, hoping to be able to pass across the ice pack and bring help. The region where they were situated is one of the least known parts in the Spitzbergen Archipelago. It has been visited only by Dutch and Swedish whalers and is composed of a number of small islands, most of them quite mountainous and almost impossible to reach.

General Nobile and the five members of the crew who had been thrown from the dirigible had made a camp on the floating ice which was in danger of breaking up at any time. Three other members of the party had left on foot in a chance effort to reach the mainland and had disappeared. No one knew what had become of the seven who had remained in the dirigible. Food supplies were running low. Two of the party had broken legs and the radio messages became weaker and more desperate. The first attempts to reach them by flying resulted in failure. General Nobile wirelessed that the one tent of the party had been painted red, so that the aviators might see it against the white of the ice. Two seaplanes had arrived from Italy to assist the Swedish and Norwegian planes. Roald Amundsen, greatest of explorers, who had quarrelled with Nobile after the flight of the year before, with characteristic unselfishness and courage secured a French seaplane and took off on a rescue flight. The heavy fogs and constant storms hampered the rescuers.

At the end of a month the relief of the lost men seemed as far away as ever. The difficulties became more apparent when it was learned that General Nobile had seen two Norwegian flyers, Captain Riiser-Larsen and Lieutenant Leutzow Holm, flying above their camp, but the two aviators returned without having discovered the explorers. It remained for a fellow Italian, Major Maddalena, flying an Italian seaplane to locate General Nobile. Three times the stranded men had seen the planes in the sky above them, and three times the planes had vanished over the grim northern horizon, without locating them.

The flight of the Italian ship was carefully directed by pre-arranged wireless signals, and on the twentieth of June Maddalena succeeded in sighting the camp and dropped 650 pounds of food and supplies by parachute. The Italian aviator reported that

there seemed to be no possibility of making a landing, and that great fissures were breaking the ice in
all directions.

In the meantime, no word had been received from
Amundsen, in the French plane flown by Rene Guil-
baud.

Even after sighting the lost men conditions remained unfavorable. The icebreakers had been
frozen in. The dog teams had been held up by storms,
and the five planes, two Norwegian, two Italian, and
a Swedish seaplane had discovered no method of
landing, because of the broken ice. Major Maddalena
made a second trip, crossing above the party eleven
times, at very low altitudes, and dropping small
parachutes to which were attached packages con-
taining spirit lamps, rubber boots, guns, cigarettes
and food. The Swedish rescue expedition under Commander Lundborg also located the explorers and
dropped additional supplies. This plane then explored the coast about Cape Leigh Smith in an attempt to find the three men who had left the Nobile
expedition on May 30, in an effort to reach land by
foot. No trace of them was found and no word had
been heard of the seven men who had drifted away
in the disabled *Italia*. On June 24, listeners at Kings
Bay received a desperate message from General Nobile that the ice had begun to break up and drift
northward. Captain Lundborg in one of the greatest
exhibitions of flying skill and courage, equipped his
plane with skis and made a successful landing. He

discovered that General Nobile had a fractured leg, and placing him in the plane successfully executed a take-off and flew to Hinlapen Strait where another Swedish plane took him to the base ship the *Citta di Milano.*

Returning on an attempt to rescue the other men the plane crashed on landing, and although the pilot escaped injury the ship was damaged to such an extent that it could not be repaired. General Nobile had very little to add to what was known concerning the missing members of the party. He said that the dirigible had left after the crash and drifted eastward a distance of about ten kilometers, then the watchers saw a burst of dark smoke and flame, and the dirigible vanished. He knew nothing of the three men who had attempted to reach land on foot.

As this book goes to press the world awaits the outcome of the continuing efforts to rescue the men left on the floe, to locate Amundsen, and his five companions, and some word of the lost members of the *Italia's* crew. Their fate may never be known. Perhaps the resources, the skill, and the unselfish heroism of pilots of all nations may enable the airplane to write a glorious chapter in the history of aviation, by being the instrument of rescue.

CPSIA information can be obtained
at www.ICGtesting.com
Printed in the USA
BVHW041042160223
658635BV00014B/160